THE INTERN'S MANIFESTO

HOW TO SURVIVE YOUR FIRST EVER OFFICE JOB

MATTHEW CROSS

PORTICO

~~You don't have to be mad to work here,~~
~~but it helps.~~

Great acts are made up of small deeds.

LAO TZU

First published in the United Kingdom in 2014 by
Portico Books
10 Southcombe Street
London
W14 0RA

An imprint of Anova Books Company Ltd

Copyright © Portico Books, 2014

ISBN 978 1 90939 650 0

A CIP catalogue record for this book is available from
the British Library.

10 9 8 7 6 5 4 3 2 1

Printed and bound by 1010 Printing International Ltd, China
Illustrations by Colin Elgie

This book can be ordered direct from the publisher at
www.anovabooks.com

CONTENTS

Re: YOU
FAO: YOU
Subject: YOU

DEAR YOU

CONGRATULATIONS ON SUCCESSFULLY BECOMING AN INTERN! YOU'VE DONE WELL TO GET THIS FAR. YOU ARE THE BEST OF THE BEST OF THE BEST.

BUT DON'T KID YOURSELF, THE REAL HARD WORK IS YET TO COME. YOU MAY HAVE SURVIVED SCHOOL BULLYING, WEDGIES, ACNE, STUNTED GROWTH, BEING DUMPED BY YOUR FIRST LOVE, UNIVERSITY EXAMS AND 10-HOUR SHIFTS AT THE LOCAL McDONALDS, BUT YOU HAVEN'T EXPERIENCED PROPER MISERY, TORTURE AND HARD WORK UNTIL YOU'VE WORKED AS AN INTERN IN AN OFFICE.

WELCOME TO THE WORLD OF THE INTERN'S MANIFESTO – YOUR ULTIMATE GUIDE TO LEARNING ALMOST EVERYTHING YOU NEED TO KNOW TO BECOMING THE GREATEST INTERN EVER.

AND IF THAT SEEMS TOO MUCH LIKE HARD WORK, DON'T WORRY. JUST SURVIVING FROM DAY TO DAY IN THE OFFICE ENVIRONMENT WILL STILL FEEL LIKE A MASSIVE ACHIEVEMENT.

THE ROAD TO INTERN ENLIGHTENMENT BEGINS HERE. SO STRAP YOURSELF IN, IT'S GOING TO BE A BUMPY RIDE …

INTERN CHECKLIST

Feeling anxious about your future? ☑

Don't know what you want to do with your life? ☑

Wish you were still at university? ☑

Too old to live at home with your parents? ☑

Worried that your friends all seem to know what they're doing? ☑

Want a career all your friends will be jealous of? ☑

Looking for exciting challenges in a lively and fast-paced environment? ☑

Not motivated by money? At all? Seriously? ☑

Heard about interning but don't know where to begin? ☑

Your dad's bought you this book as a Christmas present, because he no longer wants you living in his house? ☑

ABOUT THE AUTHOR

I know what you're thinking. Who the hell does this guy think he is, trying to teach us, inform us and entertain us by writing a book about the confusing and little-known world of interning? Well, why don't I tell you a little about myself to make you feel more at ease. I do feel slightly responsible: by reading this book, you have inadvertently placed your career in my hands, and I don't really want to be responsible for giving you bad advice or, worse, putting you off from following your dreams. When it comes down to it, I'm a nobody as well. No one listens to me. My mum still buys my socks. Yes, I've written this book – but I'm not a millionaire. In fact, if you've got a couple of quid you could lend me until the end of the month that would be great.

However, I have been an intern. And not just once, but a few times, in various places. I've done a couple of one-week placements at newspapers, a six-week work experience stint for a big-name magazine and survived being a publishing intern for a whole year. I've got the credentials. I've done my tour of duty.

So, think of me as your own personal war reporter, caught in the war zone, heroically sending back the truth of what life is really like in the real world of modern offices. Look on me as your experienced man in the know. The guy who can unlock doors. I want you to think of me as the guy who has been there, done it and bought the T-shirt. And then ripped the T-shirt up!*

After graduating from Nottingham University with a Masters degree, I spent a few years as a music and film journalist working for various magazines and newspapers. At the age of 24, I applied for an internship at a music-publisher's book division via the *Guardian Jobs* section. I got the job after four haunting interviews and have never looked back. To this day, I believe getting this year-long internship was the best thing that ever happened to me – it focused my thoughts like a laser beam on what I wanted to do with my life. It honed the skills that I wanted to learn and made me think about who I wanted to be. I later found out that over 500 applicants applied for the same internship role and the person who came in second position is now one of my best friends. I suppose what I am trying to say is that getting an internship may seem like lots of hard work (and it is) but, once you do, you may just be rewarded hugely for it.

TESTIMONIALS ABOUT THE AUTHOR AS AN INTERN

'Matthew was the only intern we ever had. So we assume he was great – it's hard to tell when you have nothing to compare against.'

'Michael, who? Matthew? Oh, yeah, the intern – I remember that guy. Where's he now?'

'The intern? I know him – he still owes me fifty quid.'

'Matthew made the best cup of tea ever.'

'He liked biscuits, that's for sure.'

'Nice guy. Good body. Tell him to call me, next time you see him.'

---

*In fact, on that note, while I've got you here, I'd like to take this opportunity to mention www.internstuff.com, my one-stop merchandise website that sells top-quality, hand-made and affordable stuff for all aspiring apprentices and interns. It's become the internet's number one website where you can order and buy amazing T-shirts, mugs, pens, calendars, etc. with witty slogans on them like 'World's Greatest Intern', 'I Survived Being An Intern', 'Intern ... And Proud' and 'I interned at [insert company name] and all I got was this lousy T-shirt!'. The website is www.internstuff. com and if you quote code BOOK1, I'll give you ten per cent off**

**For all sales over £250.

CHAPTER ONE
WAKE UP!

IT'S TIME TO GET READY FOR WORK

You're an intern. Congratulations. Despite how hard it felt getting to this point, the hard part is still left to come. Surviving an office job is stressful enough, but being the intern – the lowest paid and least respected member of the workforce – is even harder. But don't worry – you have youth, good looks and cheerful enthusiasm on your side. Let's celebrate those first baby steps towards becoming employed and, therefore, a valuable member of society.

BEST INTERN ADVICE EVER #1

Never turn up late and just say, 'Sorry, but I overslept.' That's rubbish. Always blame the trains.

HOW TO BECOME AN INTERN

I'm guessing that because you bought this book (or, more likely, somebody bought this book for you) you are either a) interested in becoming an intern, b) keen to learn more about becoming an intern, c) curious as to what an intern does, or d) already have an intern placement lined up and this book popped up in Amazon because it has 'intern' in the title and you had a tenner spare in your account.

There are many qualities you need to become an intern: the main factor obviously depends on your enthusiasm and passion (and desperation) to gain vital work experience during or after your university or school career. And there are many online avenues you can explore to find out the best places to be an intern. But first you need to do one simple thing:

YOU HAVE TO DECIDE WHAT YOU WANT TO DO FOR THE REST OF YOUR LIFE.

That's it.

Honestly, this is your biggest challenge. Once you've nailed this, everything else will sort-of fall into place. So...

- WHAT INTERESTS *YOU*?
- WHAT DO *YOU* LOVE TO DO MORE THAN ANYTHING ELSE?
- WHAT CAREER DO *YOU* WANT?

For instance, if you want to become a vet, proactively investigate local zoos close to you and look up veterinary schools and practices in your area – reach out to them and enquire if they offer any work experience or internships. Speak to the local vet, pop in to see them armed with loads of questions. If you want to work in fashion, visit ukfashionintern.com. If you want to intern in publishing, keep your eyes peeled for Google alerts or the jobs section of the broadsheets.

At the risk of sounding flippant, deciding *how* to become an intern is UP TO YOU. This book is your guide to help you once you've become an intern. There are so many ways of getting internships these days that to explain them all would fill this book. Use the internet as your first point of call – see what's out there and what's not. I don't know what your career dreams are, so it's hard to tell you how to achieve them. All I can tell you is that THERE ARE SO MANY OPPORTUNITIES OUT THERE that the only thing HOLDING YOU BACK IS YOU.

The hardest decision to make regarding your career once you graduate or are ready to take that first step up on the career ladder is the first one: working out what job you would like to do for 40-plus years of your life. If you know this, great. You can begin. If you don't – DON'T PANIC. At the back of this book is a section on websites and books to check out that will help find the right path for you.

QUOTES TO MAKE YOU SOUND EVEN MORE EDUCATED

I learned the value of hard work by working hard.

MARGARET MEAD

NAMES OF INTERNS

Your co-workers will have a habit of not remembering (and misremembering) your name, even though it's a cardinal sin (which they'll always remember) if you forget theirs. As a Matthew, I was forever remembered as Michael or Martin (and still am) – and I used to respond to both, instead of correcting them.

For the first few days of your internship people won't take the time to remember your name. Instead, you'll end up being known by one of these beauties below instead. But don't worry, once you do a good job and start getting a reputation for being a hard worker, everyone will want to know your name. But be careful, these nicknames could stick...

- Lackey
- Minion
- Pawn
- Flunky
- Slave One
- Tea-boy
- Teasmaid
- Tea-machine
- Trainee
- Runner
- Newbie
- The intern
- The new girl
- The new boy

- A scrub
- The 'New John'
- The 'New Lucy'
- The kid
- Champ
- You there
- Oi
- Tricky Dickie (if your name is Richard)
- Babs (if your name is Barbara)
- Dave (if your name is David)

- Little Lord Fauntleroy (if you're posh)
- Cameron (if you look like Cameron Diaz, for example)
- Charlie (if you look like Charlie Sheen, for example)
- Mate / girlie
- Chap/Chapess
- Darlin'/Sweetie

THE SIX THINGS YOU MUST DO BEFORE YOUR FIRST DAY AS AN INTERN

Before you wake up on your first day of being an intern, may I just remind you of the six things you needed to have done before this point. I'm sure you've already done them – you seem like you have your head screwed on in the right place. But just in case you haven't ... just in case you forgot ... just in case you have no ruddy idea what you are doing, let's just quickly go over them, shall we?

1. CREATE A LINKEDIN PROFILE (WWW.LINKEDIN.COM)

Linkedin – let's be blunt about this – is 'the work Facebook'. You may never check it, you may check it all the time, but it's useful to have set up so that in the first week of meeting everybody, you can then immediately create connections with people at your work placement. Don't worry if your profile is light on experience or connections, just focus on filling it up with as many useful and relevant skills, experience and hobbies as possible. Unlike Facebook, it all counts. Once you gain more experience and more internships, jobs or placements you can start deleting your older jobs. Try and connect to as many people as you can, as early as you can – especially if your internship is shorter than a month. Pretty soon all those connections will add up and you'll start noticing how everybody in business knows everybody else. Employers of the future will gaze upon your Linkedin profile with wonder at all your connections, so get in early and do this NOW!

2. START A BLOG AND SET UP A WEBSITE
If you're a creative (writer, designer, etc.) person you may already have a website or blog that you update regularly. If so, great. If not, get one up and running quick-smart. This is a great opportunity for new people – who will be fascinated by who you are anyway – to check you out in more detail, without having to ask you directly. And, who knows, they may start regularly reading your work and passing it on.

3. INVESTIGATE THE COMPANY YOU'RE INTERNING FOR
This is vital. In fact, I don't know why I didn't stick this at Number One. Print off the company's history, details, products, staff structure, motto – all the juicy stuff that most companies display proudly on their website. Also, do a Google search for any negative associations with the company, for example, you may find an article labelled 'So-and So Company MURDER intern number five', in which case, you may want to call in sick.

4. JOIN RELEVANT CLUBS OR EVENTS
Whatever and wherever your intern placement and no matter for how long you are doing it, it's always productive to sign up, join or tag along to a relevant club, event or venue; it may help you learn more about that industry sector, and also lets you meet like-minded souls.

5. THINK ABOUT WHAT HAPPENS NEXT

Before you begin your internship, have an idea (and it only needs to be an idea) about what you're going to do when it ends. If the work experience is only one week long, make sure you have plans to keep inspired and proactive afterwards to keep your mind focused.

6. CHECK THE WEATHER

Seriously, this is important. I forgot to do this and on my first day got drenched right through to my bones and had to walk round the entire office and meet all my new co-workers looking like a drowned rat.

THINGS YOU'LL NEED ON YOUR FIRST DAY

This might feel like I'm stating the obvious here, but the reality is that on your first day of your new work placement you might be simply too busy preparing breakfast and making sure your clothes look smart (see page 73) to focus on the little things you'll need to get you through. These are the essentials.

- An over-the-shoulder bag (don't use your smelly gym bag).
- A pad of lined paper (for making notes, obviously).
- Post-It notes (just in case they're not provided – they always come in handy).
- A piece of fruit (this will make it look like you take care of yourself).
- Lunch (preferably home-made the night before).
- A selection of pens (blue, red, highlighters – whatever you fancy).
- The book you are currently reading (even if you don't have one or hate to read, take an impressive book with you and flash it about when you take it out of your bag – let everybody see that you're a reader and what you're into).
- iPod, iPad or mp3 player (just in case you're placed up in the loft filing tax returns and invoices and need some light relief)
- A commuting timetable (make sure you have a list of train or bus timetables so you can avoid having to wait around for hours after a stressful day).
- Spare shirt (just in case you spill something, get wet or dirty)
- Newspapers (if anything has been reported in the press that is relevant to your internship or company, take the newspaper in and flaunt it at the appropriate time.

QUOTES TO MAKE YOU SOUND EVEN MORE EDUCATED

It is the working man who is the happy man.
It is the idle man who is the miserable man.

BENJAMIN FRANKLIN

COMMUTING – DO'S AND DON'TS

Commuting to the office, you'll find, is a big part of your day. Cycling to work – if you can – is the ideal. It's the best way to prepare psychologically for a hard day's work, as well as an amazing way to unwind after a long day – exercise will promote the release of endorphins in your body, helping you de-stress and feel good.

However, for the 75 per cent of the world who don't/can't cycle to work then it looks like you're stuck with the following alternatives: a) bus, b) train, c) car, d) walk.

If you can walk to the office, then you're lucky. Don't take it for granted. Not only do you get an extra hour in bed – for which your co-workers will hate you – you also avoid the stress of waiting with the rest of the rats for a train (which has been delayed or cancelled), waiting for a bus (which has been delayed or cancelled), or driving a car (which will be inevitably delayed by traffic).

In order to prepare you for your daily commute, I've devised this list of things to watch out for – stuff that is most likely to put you in a foul mood for the rest of the day.

THINGS THAT WILL DRIVE YOU MAD ON YOUR DAILY COMMUTE

- Seeing the same people every single day and never speaking to them.
- Being crammed like sardines in a space designed for humans.
- That person who always goes crazy if they miss the train/bus by one second.
- The people who scream, 'CAN YOU MOVE DOWN PLEASE!' when there is nowhere to move down to.
- Getting your hand/leg/other body part caught in a closing door.
- Forgetting your travelcard or bus ticket and having to pay for a new one.

- Getting stuck next to the man on the bus with terrible body odour.
- Falling asleep and missing your stop.
- Giving up your seat for a pregnant women, only to find out she's not pregnant, just fat.
- Your boss never believing you when you call to say you're running late because your train has been delayed or cancelled.

It's not all bad, though. Sometimes your commute in can be relatively enjoyable.

THE POSITIVE SIDE OF COMMUTING

- You can shut out the entire world by watching a movie/listening to music on your smartphone.
- You can fall asleep against the window and get an extra 45 minutes' kip – just make sure you wake up in time to get off.
- You can flirt outrageously with/ogle the boy/girl you fancy.
- Use the opportunity to catch up on 'life admin' (this usually involves replying to your mum's text from three days ago, texting friends about plans and writing to-do lists).
- You have ample time to apply make-up/do your hair/floss
- Send work emails before 9am – your co-workers will be very impressed.
- Have breakfast – usually a banana.
- Read the newspaper and rip out any news stories that are relevant to your work (this will show your boss how current and 'with it' you are).
- Read a book; 30 per cent of all commuters still read a book – usually the same one that's popular at that time.
- Sit and stare out the window (if you get a seat) and just completely turn your brain off.

WHAT IS AN INTERN?

I'm hoping that you know what an intern is, right? Obviously, readers of this book will have varying degrees of intelligence – some of you will be bright sparks and finish reading this book in under an hour, some of you will take all day to get to page five, and some of you will never open the book and instead use it as a coaster. But I'm hoping that before we begin we all know what an intern actually is? So we are all on the same page before we start, here's the definition in black and white for you.

Intern (*noun*), a student or trainee who works, sometimes without pay, in order to gain work experience or satisfy requirements for a qualification.

Of course, this isn't strictly true, now is it? Modern internships, like interns themselves, differ greatly from one industry to the next and are incredibly complicated affairs. Some are one week long, some a month, or three months or a year. My internship lasted a year and was designed as a 'fast track' experience of the many areas that come together to form the publishing industry. Within that one year, the intern was to spend time in every area (legal, editorial, design, sales, production, accounts etc.) at one particular company to learn as much as possible as effectively as possible. The intern could then choose which particular area he or she would like to concentrate on most.

Of course, not all internships are like this. Many years before this particular internship, I was an intern at a magazine for one week. This wasn't meant to provide much training or on-the-job learning of certain skills. It was designed more as an insight into how one particular company in one particular industry works, and to provide more experience on a CV. Interestingly, it was that one week as an intern that helped my CV stand out a little more than others during my later internship placement application. Every little helps.

So, let us expand the definition. An intern is:

1. Someone who usually wants to explore many options for their next job, or career in general.
2. Most likely to be unpaid.
3. Likely to still be at school or university, or a recent graduate.

While interns themselves are unique human beings, a company that hires paid interns in this global economic climate is also becoming rarer. However, a company that does promote and encourage internships does so because:

1. It often has a special project in mind that is a good fit for a part-time employee.
2. It knows it's very likely the intern will work or study elsewhere after their internship ends.

The exploitation of interns is unacceptable.

DAVID CAMERON, 2013

WHAT'S THE POINT OF BECOMING AN INTERN?

Just in case you aren't sure why you're becoming an intern, ask yourself this question (tick all the answers that apply). *Why am I becoming an intern?*

A) I felt like I should ☐

B) To get on the career ladder ☐

C) Money – plain and simple ☐

D) Fulfilling personal ambitions ☐

E) I like being around other people ☐

F) To learn new skills ☐

G) My mum and dad told me to get a job ☐

H) Intellectual gratification ☐

I) I'm tired of my friends; I need new ones ☐

J) To make people proud of me ☐

K) To get out of the house ☐

L) I'm bored ☐

M) To contribute to society and the economy ☐

If you answered (b), (d), (f), (h) and (m) – YOU DID WELL.
If you answered (a), (e), (g) and (j) – YOU DID QUITE WELL.
If you answered (c), (i), (k) and (l) – YOU FAILED MISERABLY.

HAVE YOU GOT WHAT IT TAKES TO BE AN INTERN?

While this book will endeavour to give you all the information you require to be informed, get ahead and be the best intern possible, the reality – as with any job – is that it's all down to practice, routine and not making the same mistake twice.

Before we continue any further, let's find out what type of personality you are and whether you've got what it takes to be a world-class intern. Get your pencils ready and start ticking your life away...

		YES	NO
1.	You are almost never late for your appointments.	☐	☐
2.	You like to be engaged in an active and fast-paced job.	☐	☐
3.	You are usually the first to react to a sudden event, such as the telephone ringing or an unexpected question.	☐	☐
4.	It is in your nature to assume responsibility.	☐	☐
5.	You trust reason rather than feelings.	☐	☐
6.	You spend your leisure time actively socialising with a group of people, attending parties, shopping, etc.	☐	☐
7.	You usually plan your actions in advance.	☐	☐
8.	You know how to put every minute of your time to good purpose.	☐	☐

9. You readily help people while asking nothing in return. ☐☐

10. You often contemplate the complexity of life. ☐☐

11. After prolonged socialising you feel you need to get away and be alone. ☐☐

12. You often do jobs in a hurry. ☐☐

13. You frequently and easily express your feelings and emotions. ☐☐

14. You tend to sympathise with other people. ☐☐

15. You rapidly get involved in the social life of a new workplace. ☐☐

If you answered YES to every single question, congratulations, you can turn the page and begin. A new life awaits...

If you answered with a few NOs, don't worry, just think about how you can change some of the NOs to YESes. Being an intern doesn't require you to be a perfect human specimen, but being able to identify your strengths and weaknesses is essential. As an intern, your personality will be assessed, interrogated and often rejected by colleagues and peers, so it's always best to admit to your faults first and try to address them.

If you answered NO a lot, then you may want to consider another career path. No matter who you work for, where in the world you are based and who your colleagues are, being an intern is ruddy hard work, with little reward, and very unglamorous. It's not the professional party bus you might think it is.

If you answered NO to every single question, then congratulations! You don't need this book – life has other plans for you. You're not meant to be caged in an office like the rest of us. You're free! So why not take a bath, relax, or go for a nice long walk. You're too good for this book.

TOP FIVE SKILLS YOU NEED TO BE A GREAT INTERN

I'm sure you have natural charm in spades. I'm sure you ooze it from every pore. I'm guessing you're beautiful too. In fact, I bet you're the most stunning person in any room you walk into. I'm also sure you're super-bright, the most intelligent person you know, always right and never wrong. I'm convinced you are totally confident – 100 per cent positive of everything you do – and know exactly where you're going in life and how to get there.

However, I could be wrong. You could be none of these things. You could be half of those things and simply not know it. And that's OK. You are who you are, and I'm fairly confident that you're a nice person. FYI – I am too. I'm also pretty handsome, by the way. Just saying.

Just by wanting to become an intern, this pretty much means you don't have any hidden career aspirations to become a warlord or a drug mule or a gangster – those careers, as far as I am aware, don't hire interns. So, relax, be at ease with yourself, be confident and don't worry too much.

You don't have to embody every great human characteristic in order to be a great human intern. All you need is the basic skills to get you through the first couple of weeks – the rest you'll pick up along the way.

When I started as an intern, on my first day, I was very nervous and had little confidence in my abilities a) as a human being and b) as part of a professional work environment. I had no idea if I was going to survive in an office job. But after a few days I found my feet. And so will you.

But, to help you find those feet, here are the top five skills you'll need not only to survive any office job, but also to get on your way to becoming the world's greatest intern...

1. PUNCTUALITY

For the first few days, weeks and months, the most important skill you'll need to acquire, above *everything* else, should be punctuality. And it is a skill. And I'm assuming you still love to lie-in, right?

Some people are born on time, some come out late, and some refuse to budge. Being on time is a skill you learn – so learn it well and learn it quick. Bosses and co-workers appreciate punctuality more than most other skills, if only out of selfishness – if they have to be at work on time, then so should you. If you get an intern placement at a company that plays fast and loose with these particular rules (like an advertising agency, ha-ha!) you should still arrive on time – you never know who could be watching you. And believe me, people will be watching you!

2. LEARN FROM YOUR MISTAKES

No matter what you hear from anyone – be it your boss or your mum – making mistakes is not a sin. Everyone does it. It's part of life and, more importantly, part of the fun of life. As an intern, people will expect you to make mistakes. So when you do, all you have to do is remember what the mistake was, then make a mental note and learn not to do it again. I remember in my first week of being an intern I thought I would be clever and carry a round of full-to-the-brim teas and coffees (at least eight cups) on a very small tray, across the entire office – a good 30 metres or so. Halfway to my desk, I dropped every single cup – smashing them all to many pieces, and creating a right old mess and noise in the process. The tea went over computers, people's work, faces, shoes, clothes, you name it. I briefly remember an ironic round of slow handclapping. I spent the next two hours apologising to everyone 2,000 times and mopping, draining and cleaning every tea-stained item I could find. The next day, I did two trips. I never spilled tea or coffee in the office again.

3. LISTEN

This may sound like stating the obvious, and it is, but the amount of times I thought I was listening to someone important talk and then, come the end of the sentence, realised I wasn't, made me buck my ideas up pretty swiftly – listening is a skill. The amount of time wasted in an office environment going over the same old stuff is horrifying, and you'll soon learn that what goes in one ear and stays in the other, helps enormously. And if listening is too difficult (and in meetings on a Friday afternoon at 5pm, it will be excruciating) then take advantage of skill number four ...

4. TAKE NOTES

I am an avid note-taker. I write notes down every minute of the day. I rarely complete tasks because I'm too busy taking notes. My life (and house) is filled with Post-It notes, pieces of paper with scribbles on, and to-do lists glued to every wall and white space. I have so many different-coloured Post-It notes stuck to so many walls that if I was to take them down, my house would collapse. I don't take notes because I don't listen, I take notes because I am a naturally forgetful person who, erm, um, you know.

Taking notes is, quite simply, the best way to stay awake during long and often unproductive (i.e. BORING) meetings. Plus the act itself seems to impress co-workers – it looks as if you're wrapped up in the project, passionate about your work and are proactive about completing it. That's obviously not always the case – in fact it rarely is – but by taking notes you won't be the person asking 'what happened?' later on in the day. Remember this fact: the brain retains only 5 per cent of what is said after it has been said.

5. BE PROACTIVE

Before anybody ever asks you to do something, why not ask others first if it needs doing? A great intern knows when a job needs doing and doesn't just sit and wait to be asked – they just instinctively do it. (Though, I should point out, it's probably best you ask someone first, just in case – I don't want you getting fired for doing something you shouldn't have done.) So, whether the office needs tidying, or the filing sorely needs doing, or if somebody mentions a job that they can't be bothered to do, tell them you'll do it, before you get asked anyway. It's true that while nobody in an office likes a smart aleck, a busybody or brown-noser, everybody loves somebody who does their job for them, especially if you do it well. Be that person. Likewise, don't wait to be asked to make a round of refreshments – keep an eye on co-workers' drink rates and be the first to offer a top-up. The offer of a cup of tea, especially in times of stress and panic, is the simplest, easiest and most effective way to get into your colleagues' good books.

BEST INTERN ADVICE EVER #2

Go up to a person you don't usually work with or for, introduce yourself and ask them, 'Is there anything I can help you out with, while I'm here?'

FINDING THE RIGHT INTERNSHIP FOR YOU

What kind of company do you want to work for? If you have a particular company in mind, say for example, the BBC, then check out http://www.bbc.co.uk/careers/work-experience/. If you want to work for Amazon then check out http://www.amazonfulfillmentcareers.com/programs/university-programs/internship-program. Choose the type of company – or a specific company – that you want to work for and investigate online if they advertise internships or work-experience programmes. Don't work backwards by choosing an internship at a company you don't know or don't like just because it's available – choose a company you love, and hound them until they give you one.

I hounded a London-based magazine that I really wanted to work for every week, until after about two months I finally received a reply from the editor saying, 'I loved your emails – when can you start?' It was the best six weeks' work experience I ever did. It's worth a shot!

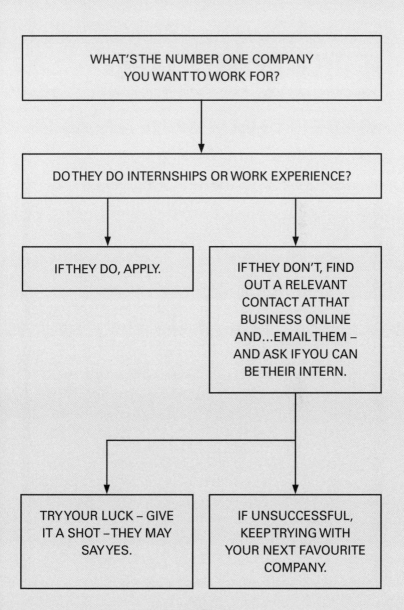

WHAT'S THE NUMBER ONE COMPANY YOU WANT TO WORK FOR?

DO THEY DO INTERNSHIPS OR WORK EXPERIENCE?

IF THEY DO, APPLY.

IF THEY DON'T, FIND OUT A RELEVANT CONTACT AT THAT BUSINESS ONLINE AND...EMAIL THEM – AND ASK IF YOU CAN BE THEIR INTERN.

TRY YOUR LUCK – GIVE IT A SHOT –THEY MAY SAY YES.

IF UNSUCCESSFUL, KEEP TRYING WITH YOUR NEXT FAVOURITE COMPANY.

A DAY IN THE LIFE

AN INTERN'S FIRST DAY ON THE JOB

A typical intern's day is far from typical. One day you could be reorganising the company's entire accounting records into alphabetical order (usually a day spent in the dusty basement), another day could be spent solely in front of the office's only photocopier – this usually involves standing in the same spot for eight hours while your head gradually slips lower and lower towards the floor until you actually doze off. Some internships are full of glamour (holding Mariah Carey's chewing gum, for example) but don't kid yourself just yet, most internships are full of the usual work drudgery that no one else in the office wants to do, so delegates it to the lowest person in the food chain – you.

Here is a pie chart of the activities you'll probably be doing in your first day on the job. Then compare this to what you'll be doing on the second day on the job. As you go along you'll see how spectacularly your role changes (or not, as the case may be).

DAY ONE ACTIVITIES

A **5%** Waiting in reception for someone to come get you at 9am

B **5%** Being told your computer hasn't been set up yet – you'll have to just sit quietly at someone else's desk for now

C **10%** Being introduced to the entire company, one by one

D **10%** Setting up your desk space

E **5%** Thinking about lunchtime

F **15%** Getting to know your team

G **20%** Offering a tea round

H **10%** Thinking about whether you have to stay late or not

I **5%** Waiting for everyone else to leave before going

J **15%** Sitting on the toilet checking Facebook

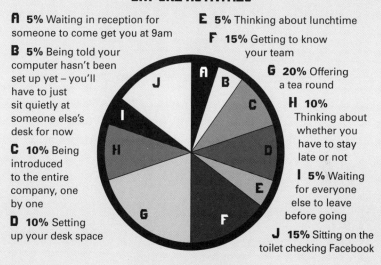

DAY TWO ACTIVITES

A **10%** Turning up 30 minutes late due to unexpectedly busy commute in

B **5%** Grovelling to the boss about lateness and feeling sick about it

C **5%** Making a tea round for pretty much everybody who works there

D **5%** Being introduced to your first task – photocopying

(it's the only job they could think of at the time)

E **10%** Trying to figure out how to use the photocopier

F **5%** Asking somebody how to use the photocopier

G **30%** Photocopying

H **30%** Sitting on the toilet checking Facebook

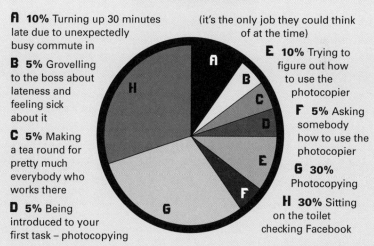

WHAT DO YOU WANT TO BE WHEN YOU GROW UP?

Before you decide where you want to be an intern, I'm afraid you're going to have to decide which dream jobs that you had as a child must be jettisoned FOREVER, because careers are like Pringles – once you pop, you can't stop. Careers are very difficult to stop once and start again once they are in motion, and it's very difficult to train to become an astronaut when you've spent 30 years as a binman. Statistically, three out of every five people in the UK want to change their job. So, think very carefully before you take your next step. Do you want to be an intern? Or do you want to be an astronaut?

Bear in mind, the percentage of you becoming an astronaut are like 0.000009 per cent – fewer than 600 people have been into space, there are seven billion people on the planet – you do the maths. The point I'm trying to make is that the chances of you acquiring your dream job is slim, unless you have seriously low expectations of yourself, so being an intern in a career path you think you want to follow is no bad thing.

According to a 2013 poll in the UK, the most *realistically* desired jobs in the UK included being a pilot, a writer, an actor, a sports trainer, a journalist, or working for a specific or unspecific charity/non-profit organisation.

Worryingly, no one wants to be doctors, nurses or bus drivers any more (yes, I wanted to be a bus driver when I was ~~fifteen~~ five). Thankfully, many of the dream jobs listed above provide scope for interns, whether it's publishing houses (writers), newspapers (journalists), theatre companies (actors, obviously) or non-profit organisations (which are currently, in the UK, a growth source of both unpaid and paid interns).

THINGS YOU SHOULD DO BEFORE YOUR INTERNSHIP STARTS

- Start getting up early (ideally, you should do this a whole week before, so your body is prepared).
- Practise being respectful to authority (maybe you could try it out on your parents, if the shock won't kill them).
- Learn how to survive on a shoe-string budget.
- Become 'advanced' in computer software like Word, Outlook, Excel, Powerpoint, etc.
- Decide who you want to be known as. If your name is Jennifer, do you want to be known at work as Jenny, Jen, J-J or The Jenster? You will be asked a million times what your preference is.
- Make plans to see all your friends *before* the internship starts. You may be too tired to do so once you've begun.
- If you can, get into a routine of doing a weekly food shop so you have all you need at home. This will save time and money during the week.
- Practise the journey to and from work a few days before you start (preferably on a weekday and at the same time of day you will be travelling at for real). Familiarise yourself with the route so you don't get lost on your first day. Just like I did.

QUOTES TO MAKE YOU SOUND EVEN MORE EDUCATED

Formula for success: rise early, work hard, strike oil.

J. PAUL GETTY

YOUR DAILY TO-DO LIST

Your entire success as an intern will be predicated on how good you are at prioritising your workload, and the best way to do this is by writing to-do lists. These lists are an intern's best friend *and* worst enemy. They're like Marmite – you either love them or hate them.

To help you out – and instead of you having to steal a notepad or write a new list out every day – why not simply photocopy my sample to-do list (that I devised during my internship) a couple of hundred times and then, throughout the day, every hour, scribble on it your list of priority jobs.

So, that's the end of chapter one. If you've made it this far, keep reading – there's prizes for those who make it to the end.

Working in an office is a continuous learning curve: just when you think you know it all, BAM!, something (or, more probably, someone) comes along and tells you you're doing it all wrong. For now, don't worry about that, let's just skip on over to chapter two, where more nuggets of knowledge await you.

NAME_____

9AM
_____

10AM
_____

11AM
_____

12PM
_____

1PM   HAVE A POO.
_____

2PM
_____

3PM
_____

4PM
_____

5PM
_____

6PM
_____

7PM   !!!!!!!!!!!!!! HOME TIME !!!!!!!!!!!!!!

CHAPTER TWO
A NASTY
PIECE
OF WORK

IT'S CALLED 'WORK' FOR A REASON...

Work is called 'work' for a reason – it's no fun. Especially if you are interning in an office environment. As the young, bright, fresh and new member of your office's workforce it's your duty to be the injection of B12 the company sorely needs. In this chapter, we look at how, with a little bit of courage and confidence, you can affect your co-workers attitudes and turn their frowns upside down. If that doesn't work, sod 'em.

WORST TIMES OF THE WORKING WEEK

A famous office joke is that you should always give 110 per cent every week you are there – Monday 50 per cent, Tuesday 30 per cent, Wednesday 20 per cent, Thursday 10 per cent, Friday 0 per cent. The truth is, the working week is fairly manageable if you know when the worst parts of it are. After a decade of working in an office, I have observed the most stressful times during an average working week.

1 = the worst / 10 = the best	AM	PM
MONDAY	1	7
TUESDAY	8	6
WEDNESDAY	4	8
THURSDAY	5	2
FRIDAY	6	9

CONCLUSION: Monday mornings and Thursday afternoons are the worst. Friday afternoons are normally the best but, occasionally, if disaster strikes – and it will – then it usually strikes around 4pm on a Friday.

TOP TEN MISTAKES YOU'LL MAKE IN YOUR FIRST WEEK

1. Spill vast oceans of tea all over something important.
2. Delete something important from the company's servers.
3. Say 'I know what that is' when you really don't. And then get caught out.
4. Call 'Jerry' John. More than once.
5. Arrive late and then make up a really bad excuse that no one believes.
6. Break the photocopier.
7. Get lost trying to find a meeting room.
8. Walk around with your fly undone.
9. Complete a project inaccurately because you were too afraid to ask what you were meant to do before you began.
10. Leave on time.

THE MANIFESTO – HOW TO BE THE WORLD'S GREATEST INTERN

Internships prepare you for the corporate world, the professional world – the Real World. If you use this opportunity to the best of your abilities, you'll set yourself up for a long and prosperous career in whatever you do.

To build upon the Top Five skills mentioned in detail on pages 24–27, here is a Skills Checklist to help you become a successful intern – no, let's get this right –THE GREATEST INTERN THE WORLD HAS EVER SEEN.

Rip this page out, Sellotape it to your desk or keep it folded up in your wallet (if you have one). Learn this verbatim – know every word by heart. Sing it to yourself in the shower. Staple it to the back of your front door so that every time you leave the house, you're prepared – mentally psyched – to show the day ahead who's the boss. I guarantee you, this manifesto will come in handy.

1. Possess the 'Yes I Can!' attitude	☐
2. Challenge yourself every day	☐
3. Ask questions	☐
4. Communicate with everyone	☐
5. Failing is OK	☐
6. Prioritise and manage your workload effectively	☐
7. Find a mentor	☐
8. Find out your value	☐
9. Exceed everyone's expectations	☐
10. Have fun!	☐

This is the intern's manifesto. All you have to do is learn it and obey it. SIMPLES. Now let's have a look at these simple dictums in a bit more detail.

1. POSSESS THE 'YES I CAN!' ATTITUDE

Develop your Positive Mental Attitude (PMA) and allow yourself the opportunity to show off the skills that are unique to you, building up a circle of trust with your co-workers so they can depend and rely on you. Even if you find the work you do boring, JUST DO IT – earn the respect of your colleagues. Always think to yourself that every new project or job that you do teaches you something new and broadens your skill set.

2. CHALLENGE YOURSELF EVERY DAY

Don't be afraid to step out of your comfort zone. In fact, embrace the opportunity to do so! Network and socialise with your co-workers, introduce yourself to everyone and anyone, find out what they are working on and if you can help out in any way.

Finish the projects you are given quickly and accurately ... then ask for more!

3. ASK QUESTIONS

Be curious. If you are unsure of something, ask someone for clarification. Don't just sit down and worry about asking. It's better to ask questions beforehand than start a job and not be 100 per cent sure you know what you're doing. Be inquisitive about your team, your department, who to avoid, and the overall structure and hierarchy of the business – know who does what and how.

4. COMMUNICATE WITH EVERYONE

Never let people have to chase you on replies to their emails or status updates on projects you are involved with. Set aside an hour a day to reply to everyone, even if it's just 'Message received – thanks'. Once you have completed a section or segment of the task at hand, let your line manager know; keep them briefed on your progress so they don't feel they have to chase you constantly. If you are experiencing any difficulty, let members of your team/department know – they may have a handy solution that helps you complete the task quicker.

5. FAILING IS OK

You'll make mistakes – of course you will – but that's OK! I make mistakes all the time ... just ask my proofreader! But as long as you take responsibility and learn from these mistakes, no one is going to give you a hard time. Don't let your fear of letting people down hold you back from challenging yourself. You are not expected to know everything, but make an effort to learn as much as you can. If somebody does give you a roasting (and it will happen), pick yourself up and don't let it faze you.

6. PRIORITISE AND MANAGE YOUR WORKLOAD EFFECTIVELY

Deadlines are tricky bastards, so prioritise your workload so you don't fall behind. Work out what the most important tasks are and when they need to be completed by. Estimate how long you think they will take and ask someone if this is reasonable. My advice is to set your own deadline for completion of tasks a day before the actual date. By doing this, you give yourself a chance to process everything, and give your brain a chance to work out if everything you needed to do was done correctly before you submit anything for inspection. It also gives you a bit of time in hand if something unexpected crops up.

7. FIND A MENTOR

From my experience, if you are able to find someone who is willing to proactively help and encourage your career growth, then half your battle is already won. I was lucky and got a great mentor who, to this day, is still invaluable to me. A mentor will be a source of great strength, knowledge and experience to you when the time comes to discuss your future career expectations. Use this person, take advantage (in a nice way!) of their skills and experience. Flattery always helps too. As does a bottle of gin.

8. FIND OUT YOUR VALUE

What do you add to your team? What unique quality of yours helps everybody else? Figure that out and you'll be golden. Aim to overachieve, pay attention to the details, take time to think before you start a project and be confident in what you'll add to it.

9. EXCEED EVERYONE'S EXPECTATIONS

Or, to put it another way, if there is another intern at the same company at the same time, be better than them. In fact, aim to outshine even the full-time staff. Impress everyone, and they'll find it hard to let you go come the end of your placement.

10. HAVE FUN!

This manifesto may seem a little heavy, so try to remember to have fun and enjoy your time there. Remember to smile, be friendly, become a human sponge and LEARN STUFF – look as if you love being there, even if sometimes you don't. The best piece of advice I was ever given (by my dad, when I was 12) was, 'If you love your work – it stops being work.' He'd stolen this advice from a poster he saw in an art shop, but that doesn't matter – the sentiment remains the same.

REFRESHMENT RATES

As sad and pathetic as this may sound, when I was an intern I became technically skilled in deciphering how long my co-workers took in drinking their cups of tea/coffee and who drank the most. Some guzzled it down, some took their time, some let it go cold. Obviously this kind of stuff varies from office to office – the basic rule of thumb is, the busier the person, the more cups they drink. You just need to be on your toes so you can always be the first to stand up and offer to make a decent cup of tea – this will not only endear you to your fellow employees but is also a good excuse to a) get away from your desk for a valuable few minutes (but no longer than ten), b) take a sneaky peek at Facebook and check in with your friends, and c) chat to the hot girls/boys who have taken your fancy over the other side of the office.

THE THREE COFFEES A DAY RULE

I've seen good men and women get into serious trouble after they've exceeded the three-cups-a-day rule. This is my own rule, and I never break it. Any more than that and your body goes into fast-forward mode, utterly doolally. One cup of coffee a day can have some amazing health benefits (especially without milk), but too much can send you into a spin of self-regret and paranoia. Your body simply cannot handle too much of it. This is what happens if you exceed the recommended daily dose:

1. You get 'The Fear', also known as anxiety. Everything all of a sudden becomes dark, negative, paranoid and overly stressy. People have even been known to hallucinate (sounds like fun, but it's a living nightmare).
2. You'll get 'The Jitters', also known as the Fidgets. You'll become wired, restless and twitchy, unable to concentrate or relax. Very detrimental to the quality of your work.
3. You'll need a wee every five minutes, which will look very dodgy to your fellow employees.

So, stick to no more than three cups of coffee a day. I know it's not easy. In a busy, stressful and fast-paced office environment it's tempting to indulge in free coffee, but the stress and anxiety you'll feel once you go over to the Dark Side is not worth it. Have a nice cup of tea instead.

THE PROS AND CONS OF BEING AN INTERN

PROS	CONS
Little responsibility	Little responsibility
Opportunity to learn	Opportunity to learn
It's only a placement, not for ever	You'll probably be unpaid
Paid? That's better than most	... but not enough to eat *and* pay rent
You'll make industry contacts	They'll only remember you as 'The Intern'
You'll be given the 'fun jobs'	... to make up for all the really 'unfun' jobs
You'll make new friends	They'll talk about you behind your back
You'll have a job	You'll have a job
Your friends will interested in your day	You'll talk about work all the time
You'll get valuable professional experience	... of filing and photocopying
You'll learn the value of a hard day's work	... by getting up at 7am
Free stationery	Not enough space in your tiny house for it all
After-work socialising	It's still work
You'll have a landline number	Your mum will call you on it
You'll find a mentor	It'll be the boss you can't stand

SIGNING YOUR INTERN CONTRACT

Depending on the type of internship you have (one week, one month, paid, unpaid etc.), your working hours, contractual terms and the general small print of your placement can differ. However, if you're interning as a 'worker' (i.e. doing an actual job as opposed to being an 'observer', shadowing staff etc.) most companies for legal purposes will require you to sign an employment contract that outlines your duties and working hours. Working hours in the UK differ, but a usual working week is between 37 hours and 45 hours.

Before your placement begins – and if you have a contract to sign – make sure you read and understand it. This will help you acclimatise to the business jargon you will now hear every day for the rest of your working life, but also help you understand your rights and responsibilities. Here's a quick guide to dealing with your internship contract.

- Photocopy it.
- With one of those cool highlighter pens, highlight any passages or words you don't understand.
- Read the entire thing – make notes on the bigger points and absorb into your head any facts or figures that you may be called upon to remember or need on a daily basis.
- Once you've read it, speak to a parent, teacher or someone you know who may be able to help you understand the bits you have highlighted.
- Compile a list of any questions you have regarding the contract.

- On your first day of work (or before you begin, if you have sufficient time) send this list, or consult personally, with a member of the HR department and ask your questions. Make this a priority – it's productive to become wise in these matters, and not just sign your life away willy-nilly. If you are unable to speak to someone at the company for whatever reason, contact your Citizens Advice Bureau (citizensadvice.org.uk) and make an appointment at your local branch to go through it all. They are there to help in matters like this.

STATISTICING THE OBVIOUS

75 per cent of all office minions believe they can run the company better than the management. 67 per cent of those minions are actually bang on the money.

QUOTES TO MAKE YOU SOUND EVEN MORE EDUCATED

Twenty years from now you will be more disappointed by the things that you didn't do than by the ones you did do. So throw off the bowlines. Sail away from the safe harbour. Catch the trade winds in your sails. Explore. Dream. Discover.

MARK TWAIN

HOW TO SURVIVE OFFICE POLITICS

Office politics is defined as *the use of power within an organisation for the pursuit of agendas and self-interest without regard to their effect on the organisation's efforts to achieve its goals.*

Office politics in any workplace is the big white metaphorical elephant in every meeting room. It looms large over every decision (for good or bad – mainly bad), it clouds the managerial judgement and wise decision-making that helps companies make a profit, and turns strong, independent characters and personalities into weaklings. Office politics – if you witness it first-hand – is like nuclear power. It looks great up close, but you don't want any of it on your hands.

Here's my guide to surviving it, or at least keeping clear of it:

1. Have issues with the way things are done or with how decisions are made? That's great! But for Pete's sake don't tell anyone in a meeting or in writing. It's counter-productive to voice your opinions in an office environment, especially if they are better ideas than the ones the boss 'brings to the table'. If you have a good idea, 'suggest it' to another member of staff. Then they'll get the blame.

2. Try to get along with everybody. The office is full of large and small personalities (and egos). It may be easier said than done, but try to get on with each and every single one.

3. Help out. If someone asks for your input (it's unlikely), rather than be the Negative Ninny, always putting a downer on

other people's ideas, be constructive, helpful and accepting. Other people's ideas may be rubbish, but go along with them for the sake of not causing any issues later on.

4. Avoid gossip. Later on in the book I will be telling you to indulge in gossip as if you were a pig in muck – that's different – but when it comes to office politics, stay clear and

let others get the blood on their hands.

5. Don't slag the boss off. All employees like to bad-mouth the boss. And as much fun as it is (and believe me, it's hugely satisfying – especially because they usually deserve it) it can cause immense fractures between the staff – those who are loyal to the boss, and those who aren't. Which group would you rather be in?

6. Be seen not to be taking part in office politics. Even though you are the intern, don't think you're not part of the office environment. If anything, you're in the thick of it. If you look, act and smell like the type of employee who washes their hands of office politics, the chances are people won't include you in it. Be above it – but don't be smug about it.

7. Be a beacon of light in the murky darkness. The office can be an unpleasant place – full of backstabbing and lies. Set an example for the rest of the office to follow.

CORPORATE FLOW OF POWER CHART

All companies – big and small – adhere to the same corporate structure. All power runs upwards, all work runs downwards. The people at the top of the chart have the least amount of work to do, but the most amount of responsibility (in theory). Those at the bottom of the chart have the most amount of work but little to no responsibility.

Before you begin your intern placement, let's take a look at the Business Family Tree, or Corporate Flow of Power Chart, as I call it. Some people may refer to it as the Pecking Order.

By understanding this flow of power, you'll be able to ascertain who the 'Big Dog' is, and who to befriend and who to avoid. If you've ever seen the TV programme *Snog Marry Avoid?*, then it's a little bit like that. Who, at work, would you snog, marry or avoid? Or, to put it in a corporate context, who would you befriend, suck up to or stay well away from?

YOU'D NEVER GUESS - FACTS ABOUT OFFICES

One out of three employees who receive a promotion uses a coffee mug with the company logo on it. Quick, find a mug with a logo on – and make sure you use it every day!

THE BIG BOSS Swans in late, disappears early, very much likes to think s/he is in charge, but actually does very little day-to-day stuff.

MIDDLE MANAGERS / LINE MANAGERS There could be millions of these idiots, all doing the same job, each one thinking s/he is in charge but really just taking orders and delegating as quickly as humanly possible. These blood-suckers will take credit for anything.

'NORMAL' STAFF These guys do all the work, are terrified for their job security, arrive early, stay late and deeply care about doing a good job. These are the people who really run any company. In theory, each member of this group is doing just their job. In practice, they are doing the job of 19 people.

FREELANCERS Most companies employ external freelancers to prevent the 'normal staff' from becoming snowed under by the copious amounts of work they have in their in-tray. They usually work from home in their pyjamas.

JUNIOR STAFF These members of staff are usually fresh out of university and very cheap to hire. They also do the lion's share of the work that the 'normal staff' like to take credit for. These will most likely be the people you hang out with the most.

YOU The intern, the bottom of the pile, the person who gets all the basic jobs that nobody else has time for or wants to do. But you've got to start somewhere – so it might as well be here. Thankfully, if you do a good job, you will usually get the credit – nobody is stupid enough to steal the credit from the lowest paid lowest rung of the corporate ladder.

THE RECEPTIONIST This person pretty much has the keys to all the doors in the office. S/he is usually the smartest, friendliest and most decent human being there. And s/he usually has a PhD in something much better than everyone else's Mickey Mouse degrees. This person deserves your respect.

OFFICE TELEPHONE ETIQUETTE

As the intern, among your tasks will be to a) act as receptionist when staff go on lunch break, b) answer the telephone, or c) make phone calls. Most members of staff usually have a staggering amount of phone calls to make or return. This is one of the drawbacks of becoming employed – people always seem to want to get in touch with you every moment of the day. It's highly inconvenient. However, the way people conduct themselves on the phone at work (i.e. a professional manner that is polite, courteous, helpful and friendly) is very different from the way people conduct themselves on the phone with their friends and family (i.e. a 'matey' manner that is blunt, obnoxious, incomprehensible and stupid).

Obviously, with you now entering the 'professional working environment', your phone manner has to match. When you make or receive phone calls on behalf of your employers, you are now the public face of their corporate image – they will expect a high level of professional conduct and behaviour. You might not be used to this, so let's run through some examples to prepare you for taking a 'work call'.

QUOTES TO MAKE YOU SOUND EVEN MORE EDUCATED

Knavery and flattery are blood relations.

ABRAHAM LINCOLN

HOW TO ANSWER A WORK PHONE CALL

HOW TO DO IT	HOW NOT TO DO IT
'Hello'	'Wasssup!'
'Good afternoon'	'Alright?'
'This is [insert name] speaking, how can I help you?'	'What do you want?'

HOW TO ENGAGE IN CONVERSATION

HOW TO DO IT	HOW NOT TO DO IT
'How can I help you today?'	'Do you need something?'
'I'll just see if she's in...'	'She ain't in.'
'Would you like to leave a message and I'll pass it on'	'Call back later, yeah?'
'Would you like to leave a voicemail?'	'I dunno how to transfer calls. Can you ring back later in ten minutes when I'm not here?'
'I'm sorry but he's in a meeting at the moment'	'He's having a wee'
'Is there anything I can help with?'	'I can't help you – I'm just the intern'
'Would you like me to put you on hold?'	'You sound hot. So, what're you wearing?'

HOW TO END THE PHONE CALL

HOW TO DO IT	HOW NOT TO DO IT
'Thanks for your call'	'Cheers, yeah'
'Have a great day'	'Stay cool, man'
'Goodbye'	'Peace out'

It's pretty simple stuff, but to be able to flip between the two styles of conversation as appropriate is a skill you'll learn in time. Just assure me in the meantime that you'll never do what I did once. When on the phone to an important client, instead of saying 'Goodbye' like a normal human being, I said, 'love you' as if I was on the phone to my girlfriend. The response of 'Excuse me?' was fairly embarrassing. Thank God it wasn't a Skype call.

YOU'D NEVER GUESS - FACTS ABOUT OFFICES

One in every four and a half minutes of your day at work will be spent online on social networks and reading blogs. Obviously, as the intern, this number will be dramatically reduced, unless, like me, you check Facebook and Twitter predominately on the toilet, in which case that's OK – that's your own time!

THE TOP TEN JOBS YOU'LL HAVE TO PERFORM MOST REGULARLY

All internships are different. Some will require the carrying out of more complex activities than the bog-standard ones listed here and some will require more extravagant or important tasks with more responsibilities. Each internship for each industry is different. For example, if you are interning at a zoo (that's possible, right?) then one of your jobs may be 'cleaning out the monkey cage', which actually sounds a lot of fun, but probably isn't day after day, poo after poo. You could be interning at MI6 and have access to top-secret files – it could happen. However, as 75 per cent of internships in the UK are office-based, it makes sense for this list to stick to the usual suspects – the tasks that will more than likely take up 90 per cent of your working day. Don't recoil in horror just yet – I have included in this list ways in which these perfunctory tasks can be done in a 'most delightful way', to quote Mary Poppins, to help spice up and inject some excitement into these jobs and make your day a little bit more dangerous than it would normally be.

1. PHOTOCOPYING

Photocopying is often regarded as the ultimate job for any intern. It's the job everybody loves to hate. Nobody in their right mind likes standing for three hours solid in front of a machine that emits enough light to permanently damage your rods and cones.

Your first week on the job may involve photocopying large stacks of documents, projects or presentations. 'It's actually an important job,' is what your co-workers will say, with a whiff of irony. And they might believe it, but the reality is it's as dull as the proverbial ditchwater.

How to make it more fun Every 100th page, photocopy your fingers doing funny shadow-animal shapes. Moose, rabbit, dog, swan, bird – the list is endless. OK, maybe not endless – but enough to keep your brain from dripping out of your ears.

Never ever do this Photocopy your genitals. This wasn't funny in the 1980s when everyone thought it was funny and photocopiers were all the rage. If you do this, you'll get caught and fired in the same sentence.

2. FILING

Filing may appear mind-numbing – and it is. There is no way of escaping that. Especially if it's a job that doesn't really need doing, but no one else has anything better to give you. For the first company I interned at, I once had to rearrange an entire year's worth of inventory filing – hundreds of pieces of paper, hundreds of paper cuts, hundreds of hours spent alone sitting on a dusty floor reciting the alphabet over and over again. If you are asked to do any filing, make sure you remember to bring a set of headphones with you and listen to some music on your iPhone or whatever you use – just make sure no one catches you. People don't like to see you having fun working, especially as the intern.

How to make it more fun Do it backwards. If you have to file things from A–Z, do it from Z–A. Actually, I can't think of anything more exciting to help you out. Sorry.

Never ever do this Sadly, filing is not one of those jobs (like photocopying) where you can just turn your brain off. You have to apply some degree of intelligence to it – you don't want to file important documents in the wrong place or the wrong way, it kind of defeats the object of it. You have to remain alert and 'with it' when filing. So make sure every twenty minutes that you have been filing things correctly. You don't want to get to the end of it and then realise you've been doing it wrong for three hours. Take a coffee/toilet break every half an hour and put on some banging tunes in your ears (or even watch a movie) – hopefully this will reduce the burning rage, boredom and contempt swelling up inside you.

3. CLEANING THE OFFICE

Many companies schedule one day a month (it's usually a Friday afternoon, when you least expect it) when they put aside a couple of hours to tidy the office completely. As boring as it sounds, tidying the office is actually a legal requirement for every company – an untidy office can lead to fire hazards, trip hazards, and any other mind-boggling Health and Safety complaints you can think of. And no company wants to be sued by a bumbling, clumsy employee for that. But if a company employs an intern then, guess what, cleaning the office becomes your number one *de facto* role. You'll be asked to spend an hour each day roaming the office for anything that looks like it doesn't need to be there and generally tidying up other people's mess. It goes without saying that you're not allowed to create any mess for yourself.

How to make it more fun As you clean the office, whistle ironically, 'Hi-ho, hi-ho, it's off to work I go' as you do it. And then see how many people start whistling the tune themselves later!

Never ever do this Throw away something of great value. I did this once and had to spend an entire evening reprinting somebody's work so it could be sent off in time. Always double-check before you throw anything away.

4. MAKING THE TEA/COFFEE

As you might imagine, one of your daily routines will be walking back and forth to the kitchen 17 times a day to make huge rounds of tea for everybody who just so happens to be in the room at the time when somebody decides they want a cuppa. It's your job to volunteer. And it's your responsibility to get it right. The best way to make sure you get everyone's tea order correct is to create a note on your phone of everybody's unique order and save it so you never have to ask again. Sometimes the order will be very complicated and memorising it will be impossible. Bear in mind that if you get just one thing wrong, that'll be one angry colleague who will make the rest of your life a living hell. So, take my advice: ALWAYS WRITE THE ORDER DOWN.

If you work in a fancy-pants office (such as one in the financial sector or advertising) with spare money to throw at luxury extravagances, you may be asked to run down to the local Starbucks and put in a massive order which you'll then have to hand-deliver to each colleague one by one – guessing correctly who ordered what.

How to make it more fun Turn the order into a rap song – use the theme tune to 'The Fresh Prince of Bel-Air' to help you.

Never ever do this Take longer than 20 minutes. Thirsty people usually want their drink order within 10 minutes of requesting it. If they don't get it in this time, they'll consider you a failure, the ungrateful bastards. And nobody wants to drink cold coffee or tea, do they? Yuck.

5. DATA ENTRY

Large companies run on databases – whether it's a list of
numbers, client names, addresses, contact details or other
information, it's always handy to have huge amounts of this
information stored neatly and efficiently in one large document,
usually an Excel spreadsheet. These databases can take years
to create, merge or update and, considering its importance,
you'd think it would be something businesses would look
after and maintain. You'd be wrong. Most important databases
usually require updating with any number of important bits of
information, because other staff members are too lazy to do it.
So, obviously, it'll be your job to create, maintain and update
any databases that are required to keep the office running
smoothly. If you do this correctly – and even add a sprinkling of
initiative – you could end up being praised by the department
and end up in your bosses' Good Books (a good place to be, if
you like that kind of thing).

How to make it more fun Colour coding! By colour coding
certain elements in your spreadsheet or database you can create
a neon-bright document that causes temporary blindness in
anyone who opens it.

Never ever do this Delete important information by mistake.
If you are in charge of collating and compiling large amounts
of data, make sure you keep it all safely and securely backed

up. You don't want to have to admit that you deleted ten years' worth of data, do you?

6. SITTING IN ON MEETINGS

As the intern, all you'll be asked to contribute to meetings is to 'sit in' on them, take notes, learn the dynamics of who's in charge and who are the subservient underlings, keep your mouth shut about any office politics you may be witnessing, and generally just sit in the corner and be quiet.

How to make it more fun Yawning in meetings is highly frowned upon. If you look around the room during the meeting you'll witness the great lengths people will go to in order to disguise a yawn. Some people pretend it's just a large intake of air, some people cough, some use their hand, some pretend to sneeze, some use distraction by pointing out of the window and yelling 'Fire!' while some people just strain their face so much to stop it from looking like they're yawning that it makes them look like they're having a poo instead. Why not devise your own way of trying to disguise a yawn?

Never ever do this Fall asleep. Meetings, especially the long and pointless type (i.e. most of them), have a tendency to make your eyes feel heavy, especially if it's a hot and humid day and you're tired from a particularly late night. Nodding off in lectures is an achievement, celebrated and applauded the world over. Snoozing in work meetings can look a tad unprofessional, even if everybody else in the room is doing their best to stay awake too.

7. PACKING UP BOXES/STUFFING THINGS IN ENVELOPES

When I was a teenager I got a summer job. The role was titled 'Administrative Assistant', but who were they kidding? I was stuffing letters into envelopes for eight hours a day. Come the end of the summer I'd licked so many envelopes that to this day my tongue refuses to get wet – I've had the inverse Pavlovian experiment and even seeing the back of a letter makes me dizzy. As the intern you'll experience a similar feeling towards letters, jiffy bags, boxes and the like. You'll be so sick of the sound stretched parcel tape makes that every time you hear it your liver will shut down and your ears will bleed. During my times as an intern I calculated that I packed on average 20 boxes a day for 250 days. I'll let you work out the maths on that one.

How to make it more fun I never got any help with this, so I'll be darned if I'm going to give you any. You're on your own with this one. Good luck!

Never ever do this Cut your tongue on an envelope. When I did this job I used to get so many paper cuts in my mouth that I was unable to eat for days (which was fine, as I couldn't afford food anyway).

8. COVERING RECEPTION

This is actually quite a fun task and can be a bit of a break from your usual interning duties. Most receptionists need food at lunchtime, at which time you will be drafted in for one precious hour to assume their responsibilities. This will cover a multitude of fairly important tasks, such as answering calls into the office (which you then transfer to private extension lines – good luck with

---

QUOTES TO MAKE YOU SOUND EVEN MORE EDUCATED

Experience: that most brutal of teachers.
But you learn, my God do you learn.

C. S. LEWIS

---

that) as well as franking post, signing in visitors, and generally saying hello to everyone who walks past you in the hope that just one person will stop and have an actual conversation with you.

How to make it more fun When somebody calls the office, pretend there is static or bad reception on the line by making funny crackling and shushing noises. This is sure to reduce your workload considerably.

Never ever do this See above. Just in case your boss walks through the reception area and all they can hear is your crackling and shushing noises.

9. OTHER ADMINISTRATIVE MENIAL TASKS

The word 'admin' gets bandied about a lot in an office. You'll hear it a lot, for sure. It's effectively an umbrella term to describe menial tasks. Just like binmen are now called 'waste technicians', 'admin' really is just another word for 'rubbish jobs'. Other 'rubbish' duties you'll be asked to carry out are labelling files, booking meeting rooms, stationery 'runs', unpacking stationery 'runs', putting things in boxes, taking things out of boxes, cutting things out, sticking things together, going to the shops to buy people's lunch because they're 'snowed under', and, my personal favourite, writing up minutes from meetings. Yes, you'll be asked to write up the non-events that occurred during a non-eventful meeting into a document NO ONE WILL EVER READ AGAIN.

How to make it more fun As you carry out these tasks, do it in the style of your favourite character from a movie, TV show or book. For example, if you're preparing the minutes of a meeting, use 'ye olde English' to describe the events, rather than just plain old boring modern English. 'Ye boss looked betwixted at thy weekly numbers...'

Never ever do this Moan about any of it. As much fun as it is to whinge and complain about being giving menial tasks, the reality is that a lot of everybody's daily work routine is completing menial tasks. You're not alone. Besides, if you complete the boring jobs quickly and efficiently, you may find you'll be given more fascinating jobs sooner.

10. PROPER WORK

I regret to inform you that, as an intern, you won't see much of this 'proper work', i.e. the interesting stuff other people seem to be doing and the main reason why you wanted this internship in the first place. If your internship is at a fashion house, chances are you won't be designing skirts – but you may get to model them.

As people around you zip around and dash off, looking as if they are super-busy and mega-important, you'll feel shame and embarrassment that the job you're doing is nowhere near as important. Try to resist the urge to feel this way. Instead, take comfort in the tasks you've been given to do – it won't be long before your co-workers will ask more from you. Take the time to get to know your surroundings and learn what you can, so that when you do get a big job to do, you can do it well.

Besides, from what I've learned, co-workers (in particularly middle managers) love nothing more than letting you know just how difficult and/or important the job they are doing is, even if it isn't and they're not. You may yearn to get a piece of the action, but for now take one step at a time, and it won't be long before you get some 'proper work'.

How to make it more fun When and if you do get some 'proper work' it's probably best just to crack on with it as best you can without messing it up. Hopefully, the project itself will be fun enough.

Never ever do this Mess it up. If you feel like you don't understand what has been asked of you, ask questions before you begin so that when you start you know exactly what you're doing.

HOW TO TRANSFER A PHONE CALL

Press the star key, or hash symbol, no, hold down the 'trans' button. Then dial the extension you need, followed by the hash symbol, then press 9, or maybe 0, put the phone down... You know what, I still have no idea how to transfer a phone call. I'm sure you'll figure it out though. If not, dial 0 (or is it 9?) and ask the receptionist to come and do it for you.

YOU'D NEVER GUESS - FACTS ABOUT OFFICES

The modern-day office chair – the one thing you'll spend the rest of your life sitting on – was invented by naturalist Charles Darwin in the 19th century. That's right, the man who changed the world by theorising that all humankind evolved from previous species also created the office chair. Amazingly, Darwin was the first bright spark to add wheels to his chairs so he could zoom around to his laboratory specimens more quickly. Remember that the next time you sit down on your office chair!

YOUR CAREER
BY NUMBERS

Over the course of your career, expect to encounter
the following things:

- 3 genuinely horrible bosses
- 2,000,000 Post-It Notes
- 500,000 printer paper jams
- 11 broken photocopiers (all your fault)
- 20,000 paper cuts
- 170 vital company files deleted (by mistake)
- 50,000 computer meltdowns
- 12,000 pointless meetings

KILLER MOVIE QUOTES ABOUT OFFICES

*'We're adding a little something to this month's
sales contest. As you all know, first prize is a
Cadillac Eldorado. Second prize is a set of steak
knives. Third prize is you're fired.'*

GLENGARRY GLEN ROSS (1992)

CHAPTER THREE WORK LIKE A CHARM

YOUR PLACE IN THE OFFICE

You've made it this far! To awkwardly paraphrase Darth Vader, 'Impressive. Most impressive. But you're not a Jedi, yet.' Yes, becoming a great intern is a lot like becoming a Jedi. You'll be sent to train somewhere far away and remote (usually Swindon), there'll be lots of heavy lifting and you may be humiliated by an elderly figure with a speech impediment. And while the rewards won't be anywhere near as significant, you won't have to kill one of your parents at the end. Though if you're still living at home, you may feel like it.

THE EVOLUTION OF THE WORKING WEEK

The working week, as you'll discover, can drag on a bit. We human beings – and I'm including you in this – haven't always worked a 40-plus hour week though. In fact it's a fairly recent invention. For a couple of thousand years before you were born, the rest of the world enjoyed periods of intense laziness, followed by periods of super-activity, which nobody enjoyed. The working week as we know (and hate) it now has evolved and fluctuated over the years into the steady, perfunctory beast we dread every Sunday night. Sadly, I doubt it will ever change back again.

During the Roman Empire, around the fourth century AD, people who had jobs to go to worked for 190 days – leaving them with a whopping 175 days of holiday per year. Although, it's not like they had Disneyland or anything fun to do on their days off.

In the Middle Ages, around 1,000 years ago, people who had jobs (as well as chronic syphilis) worked six days a week, eight hours a day – but had no holiday, so worked 300 days a year, on average.

In the US around 1800, it was not unusual for men and women to work 14-hour days – but they had the Industrial Revolution to blame, so at least they were busy for a good cause. In 1840, when the US President Martin van Buren got sick of working long days, he reduced the average working day to 10 hours.

It wasn't until the 1930s that the eight-hour working day came into existence – Henry Ford, a former intern himself, usually gets the blame – but it was the US's Fair Labor Standards Act of 1938 that generally is considered as introducing and establishing the five-day, 40-hour working week. With the US being the world's largest superpower at the time, the rest of the Western world was pretty much forced to follow suit.

Right here, right now, in the 21st century people in the UK go to work on average 252 days per year – making the UK one of the longest-working nations in Europe. In the US it is slightly higher at 262 days a year – but their average is based on a 35-hour working week, in theory.

In the UK and the US, the maximum hours you can work in any job – contractually – is 48 hours per week, according to the Working Times Regulations.

Of course, this is all in theory. As you'll discover, most colleagues and other employees continually work over and above their contractually obliged working hours. This is not usually due to any loyalty to the company, more usually it's out of fear that there are simply not enough hours in a day to get all your work done.

TGI FRIDAY

As you'll discover, a professional workplace environment on a Friday is very different from a professional workplace environment between Monday and Thursday. There's less tension and stress in the air. Deadlines are more relaxed – everything that needs to get done gets shifted to Monday all of a sudden – and overall there's a much more exciting, fun, livelier and positive atmosphere to be in. While this isn't strictly true for every workplace (hospitals, I imagine, are pretty intense every day) – and not in any way condoned by your employers – the old Chinese proverb 'TGI Friday' is certainly one that rings true for every employee (including you) who has had a hard week. As the intern you'll notice a sudden shift in playfulness among your co-workers; they won't be so stressed out and manic; hell, they may even sit back in their chairs and ask you what your plans are for the weekend.

Even though they're prone to 5.30 disasters, overall Fridays in offices are the best days of the working week, for sure. To celebrate this fact, over the past ten years I have observed the following naturally occurring statistics at workplaces on this day:

- Productivity on a Friday drops by 45 per cent.
- Non-work-related internet searches increase by 65 per cent.
- Lunchtime breaks increase from 60 minutes to 90 minutes in length.
- Lunchtime meals include alcohol.
- Meetings on Friday are shorter by 25 per cent.
- 50 per cent of the workforce doesn't turn up.
- Of the 50 per cent of the workforce that does turn up, 30 per cent turns up between 9.30am and 10.45am.
- From 1.30–5.30pm, 90 per cent of the 50 per cent who have turned up are 100 per cent thinking about Friday-night plans and not work.
- Conversations about weekend plans overtake conversations about workload.
- Conversations in general increase by 50 per cent.
- Post-breakfast and post-lunchtime chocolate snacking increases by 70 per cent.
- Conversations about chocolate snacking increase by at least 30 per cent.

OFFICE JARGON YOU'LL HAVE TO LEARN

When you're at university, or at college or school, the way in which you communicate with your friends is very important. The words you use, how you say them and what you don't say are all 'verbal signifiers' that reflect and suggest your overall empathy, compassion and emotions towards other human beings. In a workplace, it's different. Here, words are nothing more than meaningless vessels continually transporting pointless streams of incomprehensible jargon from one confused mouth to another, until it gets to the point where you step away from a conversation and have no idea who said what or what actually needs to get done. No matter what industry you have entered or what type of internship you are on, as long as you are in an office or corporate environment, the jargon remains the same.

If this all sounds rather worrying and confusing, don't panic, that's what I'm here for. Here's a quick guide to some of the more confusing corporate 'lingo' that most of your co-workers – in particular middle managers – will use most of the time without any care or consideration as to its etymology or meaning.

NOT ENOUGH BANDWIDTH

Example 'Sorry, Steve, I don't have enough bandwidth for that.'
Reality 'Steve, I might kill myself if you give me any more work to do.'

IDEA-SHOWER

Example 'Let's meet today at 2pm and idea-shower this project, yeah?'
Reality 'I've got no ideas. Let's try and come up with some very quickly.'

RADAR

Example 'It's been hectic – but you're on my radar now.'
Reality 'I've been at the pub – but now I've seen your face in the corridor, it's reminded me to do that important job you asked me to do.'

THINKING FORWARD

Example 'Thinking forward, what's our strategy?'
Reality 'I've got nothing to offer you now, so let's talk about a date in the future that we'll all forget.'

360-DEGREE THINKING

Example 'Let's 360-degree think this, team.'
Reality 'We need new ideas because all our current ones are rubbish.'

AT THE END OF THE DAY

Example 'At the end of the day, it's got to get done.'
Reality 'At the end of the day, I'm going home – you stay and finish it.'

110 PER CENT

Example 'Let's put 110 per cent into this, OK?'
Reality 'Please try a bit harder than you usually do.'

VERSION 2.0

Example 'This'll be version 2.0 – better than the original.'
Reality 'This'll be the second version, a little bit different from the original.'

TRENDING

Example 'What's trending?'
Reality 'What's popular at the moment so I can look cool with people younger than me?'

HEADS-UP
Example 'Just a quick heads-up – numbers are down.'
Reality 'I'm smugly alerting you to fear for your job security.'

ACTION
Example 'Hi, Sarah, can you action this for me?
Reality 'Hi, Sarah, I'm too cool for regular verbs, so can you accomplish this task for me?'

ÜBER
Example 'I'm über-excited about this!'
Reality 'I'm desperate to show you I care about this and 'über' seems to convey that perfectly.'

JUDGEMENT CALL
Example 'I don't want to get involved, it's your judgement call.'
Reality 'I'm scared to express my opinion – I delegate the decision to you.'

BACK IN THE DAY
Example 'Back in the day, it was totally different.'
Reality 'Twenty years ago, I still had no idea what was going on.'

MY BAD
Example 'My bad.'
Reality 'That was my fault – but by saying "my bad" I can get away without saying sorry.'

LITERALLY
Example 'I literally cannot believe that just happened.'
Reality 'I literally can't stop applying this word to every sentence I say, even though I am literally using it wrong.'

END OF
Example 'I don't want to hear your excuses. End of.'
Reality 'I need to end this declarative statement with an even more declarative statement – just so we both know I'm making my point with a declarative statement.'

AIR IT OUT
Example 'I heard you don't like the way I work – so let's air it out this afternoon.'
Reality 'We can't agree about anything – so meet me out the back of the office at 5.30pm and we'll fight it out to the death.'

AL DESCO
Example I forgot to have breakfast this morning ... so I had it al desco.'

Reality 'I forgot to have breakfast this morning, so I ate it at my desk ... but I heard someone use the term "al desco" on TV, so I've decided to use it too ... but pass it off as my own witty saying.'

DOWNSIZING
Example 'We're downsizing.'
Reality 'You're fired.'

DREJJING TO IMPREJJ

When you arrive on your first day as the office intern, make no mistake, your appearance, behaviour and personality will all be under intense scrutiny by your new fellow workers, peers, bosses and even the receptionist. Therefore it's important you remember this cliché:

FIRST IMPRESSIONS COUNT

In a professional office environment, what you say and do is essential – it really matters. However, that's only half the battle – what you wear is just as important too. IT'S VITAL YOU LOOK GOOD, especially if you're dealing face-to-face with clients or customers, or will be a visible public face of the company, for example at trade events, in open-floor offices or if the building is made entirely out of glass.

LOOK SMART

If you're a man this means, I'm sorry to say, a suit – or, at the very least, smart trousers, clean pressed shirt, buffed shoes and either a smart jumper or suit jacket. Even if your internship is at a creative office (such as a publishing company or advertising agency), most men you'll notice will dress smartly in a shirt and suit trousers, and most women will dress up, rather than down, either in smart blouse or smart trouser/shirt combo. Of course, after your first two weeks or so, you'll feel comfortable around your co-workers enough to use your initiative: perhaps smart jeans and trainers are acceptable on most days, unless you'll be involved in 'sitting in on meetings' with clients or meeting members of the public on the company's behalf. If you work in the financial sector, for example, there is no substitute for a suit. It's uniform. So, before your first day, ideally at interview stage when you first apply for the internship, scope out the clothing your co-workers are wearing to get a sense of what seems to be the most common type of fashion around the place. If everyone is wearing a skirt or a suit (women and men respectively, of course) then copy them. If everyone is wearing flip-flops and ripped jeans then, of course, purchase a pair of both forthwith. For the first month of my internship, at a creative office, I wore a fancy grey suit (the only suit I owned) every day. No one else wore a suit except executives, management and sales staff, so I imagine I looked a bit of a wally all dressed up to the nines, while packing boxes and tidying out the stationery cupboard. But to my new employers I was making the effort to look smart and professional, and that's all that counted.

RIPPED JEANS AND T-SHIRT - NO!

Aside from the fact that nobody should wear ripped jeans any more anyway – it's the 21st century, sewing machines were invented a long time ago – the ripped jeans and T-shirt look, in an office environment, looks unprofessional and many employers would take you aside and tell you off for 'doing a Bon Jovi'. Even if the internship is based in a creative environment this slap-dash approach to your appearance is – I wouldn't say 'not allowed' – severely frowned upon. And once your new colleagues have made that first impression of you, no matter how you try to reverse it, they'll still have that impression lingering in their mind for months to follow. When I worked at a newspaper in London, I grew my hair shoulder-length, but still had to wear a smart suit – yes, I was rocking the rock-chic look *and* business-smart *at the same time*. Try imagining Kurt Cobain in a Hugo Boss suit – it just doesn't work, does it? Smart jeans and a non-threatening T-shirt are always the preferred 'safe' look that will work in your favour – and not against you – day in, day out.

IRONIC T-SHIRTS

There is an office trend at the moment – among young males, at least – for sweary, threatening or 'ironic' T-shirts, with witty/dumb phrases on them. You've seen them. They're the T-shirts with 'PLACES TO GO, PEOPLE TO ANNOY', 'I'M KIND OF A BIG DEAL' or 'IRONY – THE OPPOSITE OF WRINKLY' or something along those lines. While they may be funny in hipster circles, trust me, they're not appropriate in the workplace. A friend of mine once turned up to a meeting wearing a T-shirt with a particularly rude phrase on it and was instantly sent home for the day. It wasn't the fact that the T-shirt was rude, so much as the decision to wear it to work was ill-judged. Be careful. If I were you, I would also stay clear from the following genuine, ironic T-shirt slogans that people actually wear to the office – just to be on the safe side:

- I HATE ANNOYING PEOPLE
- DO I LOOK LIKE YOUR THERAPIST?
- YEAH, WELL AT LEAST I'M NOT UGLY!
- I'M HOTTER THAN YOUR GIRLFRIEND
- STOP STARING AT MY CHEST
- YOU CAN LOOK BUT DON'T TOUCH
- WORK – THAT ANNOYING THING BETWEEN COFFEE BREAKS AND NAPS
- I SELL CLEAN URINE
- THE GUY BESIDE ME HAS NO FRIENDS
- IT'S MY JOB TO BE ANNOYING

KEEP IT TASTEFUL

Three key words to remember when dressing for any office environment are

PROFESSIONAL
SMART
APPROPRIATE

The third and final word is probably the most important. Full of young people who are stuck indoors all day and legally forbidden to have sex on the premises, offices tend to be both sexually frustrating and sexually charged environments – and if you happen to be a young, bright and good-looking intern, chances are you're going to receive the attention and flattery of your interested co-workers. After all, you're a new person to them, who can possibly be plied with old tricks. With this in mind, it's best to dress sensibly and appropriately. In the summertime – when the majority of internships in the UK actually take place

– short skirts, skimpy dresses and flattering tops may look lovely and make you feel confident, but are they appropriate attire for an intern? They're certainly not appropriate for a male intern. While you definitely want to dress to impress, don't be *too impressive*. You don't want to acquire a status for wearing revealing clothing – a reputation like that can be counter-productive (especially among other staff members who might take great delight in knocking your attire) and work against you when it comes to being taken seriously, which is the name of the game here. Again, and as always, FIRST IMPRESSIONS COUNT. So, if I were you, I'd leave the knee-length boots and miniskirt at home in the wardrobe. That goes for you too, girls.

HOW TO IMPRESS PEOPLE
(OR, HOW TO WORM YOUR WAY INTO PEOPLE'S AFFECTION)

The everyday office environment is, basically, one of the most brutally competitive places on earth. More competitive than a boxing ring, and more violent and bloody than anything you could ever do on *Grand Theft Auto V*. Your job as the intern, the newbie, is to worm your way into your colleagues' affections so much that you become the first and only person everybody wants to talk to every day. You need to position yourself as the cool kid, the smart kid, the person everyone will want to naturally gravitate towards.

There are three ways of doing this:

1. Make a good first impression
2. Stun them with your expert knowledge of everything
3. Know all the gossip

Stupid-but-important people (the ones who tend to make all the decisions) in offices tend to cling on to or befriend the intelligent and popular people to boost their own ranking and make them seem more likeable and approachable. They don't have to be popular or well-liked themselves, they just need to be seen hanging out with the popular people. Most offices have a well-defined mixture of stereotypes and clichés – it's your job to absorb all the positive qualities of every office stereotype as well as naturally give off your own infectious charm. A good way to do this (other than just being yourself, of course) is too appear smarter and more knowledgeable than everybody else.

Studies suggest (and I'm not making this one up) that 90 per cent of all workplace conversations are gossip and that 76 per cent of all work gossip is actually accurate, which technically means (I suppose) that's it's not gossiping. I'm not sure how scientists work these statistics out, but trust me, it's true.

Anyway, before we get on to the gossiping entry, here are some amazing facts for you to smartly, wittily and charmingly insert into your workplace conversations whenever you're conversing with a VIP, your boss or any other influential person. By littering your conversations with these facts, you'll appear smart and become more popular. I've divided these facts into subject areas for your easy reference – you never know what kind of conversations you'll end up having around the office's water cooler, so it's best to be prepared for any subject that might pop up.

RELIGION
'According to Genesis 1:20–22, the chicken came before the egg.'

GENDER EQUALITY (FEMALE)
'Bullet-proof vests, fire escapes, windscreen wipers and laser printers were all invented by women – who knew!'

GENDER EQUALITY (MALE)
'Proportional to their weight, men are stronger than horses.'

PETS
'Cats can hear ultrasound.'

MATHS I
'If you were to spell out numbers, you would have to go until 1,000 until you would find the letter A (not counting any 'ands').'

MATHS II
'111,111,111 x 111,111,111 = 12,345,678,987,654,321'

RANDOM
'Every day more money is printed for Monopoly than for the US Treasury.'

PARENTHOOD
'The world's youngest ever parents were aged eight and nine and lived in China in 1910.'

INSECTS
'Ants stretch when they wake up in the morning.'

SLEEP I
'The average person has over 1,460 dreams a year.'

SLEEP II
'Dolphins sleep with one eye open.'

CHEWING GUM I
'The world's oldest piece of chewing gum is 9,000 years old.'

CHEWING GUM II
'Chewing gum while peeling onions will keep you from crying.'

SPACE

'In space, astronauts cannot cry, because there is no gravity, so the tears can't flow.'

OWLS

'Owls are the only birds who can see the colour blue.'

BATS

'Bats always turn left when exiting a cave.'

WORLD NEWS I

'In Tokyo, they sell toupees for dogs.'

WORLD NEWS II

'In Chinese, the KFC slogan "finger lickin' good" translates as "eat your fingers off".'

ART

'It took Leonardo da Vinci ten years to paint Mona Lisa's lips. But she strangely has no eyebrows.'

THE BODY I

'Our eyes remain the same size from birth onward, but our noses and ears never stop growing.'

THE BODY II

'Every human spent about half an hour as a single cell.'

SOCIAL NETWORKING

'The hash key on your keyboard is actually called an octothorpe.'

Of course, once you've used all these facts up it's down to you to source more.*

---

*In retrospect, some of the facts I have outlined here might make you seem rather nutty as opposed to intelligent. I mean, what kind of weirdo keeps useless trivia like 'bats always turn left when exiting a cave' in their head? If you ever have a conversation about bats, this is a great fact. But please don't use it if you're having a conversation about knitting, or cooking. You'll look weird.

HOW TO REMEMBER A PERSON'S NAME

Over the course of your internship you will be forced to learn loads of people's names. Thankfully, 75 per cent of them will be called David, Sophie, Richard or Claire, but for the rest who aren't, then you're going to have to devise a system so that you never forget anybody's name. Because if you do, they'll never forget it. They'll also never forgive you (and will proactively ignore you every time you walk in the room) if you call them 'Roger' when their name is 'Robert'. Nobody likes to have their name forgotten, as I'm sure you'll appreciate.

Some people are better at remembering names than others. So this will either come naturally to you or it'll be ruddy difficult. Either way, why don't you give this set of techniques below a go?

Clear your head, grab a healthy snack bar (or banana – take your pick) and pay attention to these guaranteed tricks to remembering all your co-workers' names.

MEET AND REPEAT

When you meet someone for the first time and they say, 'Hi, my name is Andrew,' instead of just nodding and moving on, take the time to look at them squarely in the eyes and say, 'Hi, Andrew, great to meet you.' By plugging this name at this time, it forces the brain to make a connection that hopefully should plant the name and face in your memory banks.

WRITE DOWN THEIR NAME

If possible, after you've been introduced to someone, write their name down, who they are and any striking features they may have (glasses, big nose, flop sweat, etc.). Then memorise that list. Next time you see them, their name should pop straight into your head.

NAME ASSOCIATION

This is a great game to play with yourself. If, for example, you meet a woman called Jenny, try to associate her name with her appearance. Is she wearing a jumper? Or jeans? If so, remember her as Jumper Jenny or Jeans Jenny. If you meet a Sarah, and she works in the sales department, remember her as Sarah Sales, and picture her in your mind sailing a boat. You get the idea.

FAMILIAR CONNECTIONS

We all do this anyway, but if you meet a John, and you have a friend or relative called John, then connect the two together in your mind. Next time you see John (at work), you'll visualise the John you know, and the name John should magically spring into your brain.

BE CAREFUL

Many experts believe that one of the main reasons we forget people's names is because we don't concentrate on remembering them when we meet them. We're too interested in, perhaps, getting the introduction over and done with to actually care what their name is. So, next time you meet a new face, take care to remember their name – and hopefully you'll have a better chance of recalling it when you need to!

TYPES OF INTERN

Fashion, accountancy, publishing, film, TV, government, legal, sales and marketing, graphic design, financial, IT, medical, broadcasting, science, manufacturing, art, music, social media – there are so many types of industries that encourage and advertise for internships that to name them all here would be impossible, not to mention a complete waste of paper. This book is bad enough. There are so many opportunities available in the workplace these days, and for most of them you're just a few clicks away on the internet from finding everything you need to know about them. I'm going to assume that you know by now what type of industry you want to gain access to and I don't need to explain them all to you, right?

What I do need to explain, however, are the seven types of interns in the world. These are the intern clichés and stereotypes that have been observed making tea in offices up and down the country. All your co-workers will be familiar with each different type and will have had a (nasty) experience with at least two of them. Your job is to confound these stereotypes, break the mould, and give your co-workers a brand-spanking new type of intern that they have never seen before.

If that all sounds too much like hard work, then at least try to avoid being one of these clichés, OK?

BEST INTERN ADVICE EVER #5

Never get angry with the photocopier. Like you, it's just doing its job the best it can.

THE 'I'M TOO GOOD FOR THIS PLACE' INTERN

These guys and girls huff and puff and mope about the office and refuse to do the menial tasks (they're beneath them) and think they're better than everyone else in the office. They refuse to take advice and are constantly on their iPhone tweeting their friends.
WORST TRAIT Their 'screw you' attitude.

THE INVISIBLE INTERN

This type of intern slinks into the background, never speaks, is never around when you need them (probably too busy hiding somewhere to avoid work) and never gets involved in any conversations or events. All in all, a bit of a waste of space.
WORST TRAIT Silence.

THE BROWN-NOSE INTERN

These chappies and chappettes are over-the-top lickspittles who have no shame in being teacher's pet. The best of a bad bunch, but still very annoying.
WORST TRAIT The desperate need to please.

THE UNDER-YOUR-FEET INTERN

Forever asking stupid questions without taking the initiative, forever lost or stuck, needy, clingy and weak, these interns are continually under the feet of their co-workers, getting in the way and needing help and reassurance every five minutes.
WORST TRAIT Clinginess.

THE CLOWN

This intern is the entertainer. The practical joker. The person who will glue your phone to your desk or encase your stapler in jelly or put 10 sugars in your tea. While they may be funny for five minutes a day, it's a little too much after nine hours.

WORST TRAIT Annoying.

THE SEX OBJECT INTERN

Renowned around the office for his/her looks, the Hollywood stud/supermodel intern is never taken seriously because he or she is just too good-looking. Half of these try to overcompensate for their looks, try to be really nice and are desperate to be seen as clever. The other half flirt outrageously and use their looks to get other people to do their jobs for them.
WORST TRAIT The jealousy they inspire.

THE OVERQUALIFIED INTERN

With 17 degrees, a Masters, three years' work experience at a company more prestigious than this current one, and two summers spent caring for children in Uganda, the overqualified intern is simply too good to be there. These types put all their co-workers to shame about how little they've achieved and contrive to make you feel bad about yourself.
WORST TRAIT They're so good they make everyone else look bad.

QUOTES TO MAKE YOU SOUND EVEN MORE EDUCATED

We make a living by what we get,
but we make a life by what we give.

WINSTON CHURCHILL

OFFICE CLICHÉS TO AVOID LIKE THE PLAGUE!

If you want to avoid becoming an office stereotype – and, trust me, you do – then you're best staying well clear of the office clichés highlighted below. Coming out with just one of these phrases will earmark you personally and permanently as a moron. Your co-workers will grimace in horror every time one of these lines is spoken, so avoid them at all costs. Think of them as the office's Voldemort – they should never be uttered for fear of casting you as a social muggle.

In 2013, a survey was conducted of the UK's worst office clichés. They are listed below. Over many years spent in an office, I've also been able to observe how many times on average these phrases are used per office per day. I've therefore compiled the two lists together, to highlight just how hackneyed the phrases are.

QUOTES TO MAKE YOU SOUND EVEN MORE EDUCATED

*Be who you are and say what you feel,
because those who mind don't matter,
and those who matter don't mind.*

DR SEUSS

CLICHÉ	AVERAGE USE PER DAY
1. 'At the end of the day'	200
2. 'What goes around, comes around'	10
3. 'It's not rocket science'	5
4. 'Thinking outside the box'	30
5. 'Flogging a dead horse'	22
6. 'Don't shoot the messenger'	7
7. 'Going forward'	45
8. 'By the close of play'	13
9. 'Give you a heads-up'	67
10. 'Live and learn'	10
11. 'C'est la vie'	17
12. 'Don't put all your eggs in one basket'	23
13. 'Hit the ground running'	32
14. 'Always look on the bright side of life'	12
15. 'Suck it and see'	14
16. 'Don't look a gift horse in the mouth'	19
17. 'Don't worry, be happy'	27
18. 'I know it's a big ask'	69
19. 'I'm out'	78
20. 'There are no flies on me'	41

I once had to walk out of a room after I heard the phrase 'At the end of the day, thinking outside the box isn't rocket science.' It was too much!

HOW TO GET AHEAD BY GOSSIPING

Modern professional workplaces don't run on wit, intelligence and hard work – they usually run on gossip, sniping and hard-nosed competitiveness. But that's none of your concern. Your job is to fit in and become part of the furniture, and the best way to do that is to learn how to gossip like everybody else. Sure, I could use this opportunity to tell you not to gossip, to avoid bitching about your fellow colleagues and tell you to stop yourself from being competitive, but that's not what this book is about – this book is about how to *survive* in an office job, not become socially rejected and trampled all over.

In order to get ahead and keep up with your co-workers, you'll need this succinct but enlightening guide (see below) to learn the tricks and techniques to gossip like a pro. If you're a girl you might not need this section – you'll probably already know it all off by heart, so why don't you skip to the next entry or go and take a nap – but if you're a guy, chances are you won't have a clue about it ... and we don't want you being left behind, now do we?

My Guaranteed Guide to Great Gossiping (The 4G Process, for short) is as follows:

- Appear to be trustworthy. The more discreet you seem, the more people will open up to you and reveal their innermost (and usually depraved) thoughts.
- Pay attention to body language when somebody is talking to you – it can reveal what they really mean.

- Always be there for people. The more available you are to your colleagues, the more likely they are to 'vent' to you about how much they hate Sandra in accounts.
- Befriend the office gossip. You'll discover who this person is approximately 30 minutes after getting there on your first day. They're not hard to spot. By befriending this person, everyone will think you're always 'in the know'.
- Introduce and insert your own rumours and gossip into conversations about the things you observe – don't be afraid to spread this stuff around.
- Whether you're just walking past a group of people or making a cup of tea in the communal kitchen, always eavesdrop on co-workers' conversations. Learn what the office is talking about – and then pass it on as if you heard it first-hand.
- Remember, statistically speaking, 76 per cent of all gossip is true – so use this fact when you are spreading gossip.
- Never leave a paper trail. Don't text or send emails. Don't update Facebook or send tweets. If a saucy piece of gossip is ever linked back to you – and there is proof – you're in hot water.
- After-work social engagements are a great way for staff to blow off steam – always make sure you are invited to whatever shindigs are occurring. Don't become the person who always says 'no' to work social events. Say 'yes', and watch the gossip fall into your lap.
- If you hear a scandalous, harmful or controversial rumour (I'll let your imagination do the work on examples here) don't spread it. Gossiping is fun but malicious personal rumours or spiteful attacks are to be avoided at all times. Have fun, but don't go too far – and if you know someone who is spreading 'bad gossip', try to stay away from them. You don't want to be associated with their kind.

Overall, office gossiping is a healthy way for you to bond with co-workers over minor instances of *schadenfreude*, but never let it get out of hand. I urge you, only ever partake in gossiping for these reasons:

- You'll learn more about the company, more than at any proper staff meeting.
- You'll learn how people honestly feel about other staff members (some could be being mistreated or bullied).
- You'll feel more validated and confident in yourself knowing you're not the only who thinks the boss is a megalomaniac.
- Venting is good – it's better to blow off steam than be powered by it.
- You'll feel trusted and part of the workforce. Knowing that people trust you enough to gossip about other members of staff to you indicates a huge amount of faith.

We're getting there, aren't we? Hope you've learnt something. But seriously, if you're struggling with any aspects of your internship, or feel as if you're being bullied or harassed, don't keep it to yourself. Take the issue up with the company's HR Manager or your mentor. They'll be able to advise you in confidence and help you resolve any conflicts or concerns. Stress and anxiety are part of everyday office life, to be sure, but you'll soon discover what's healthy and what's not and if in doubt, talk to someone about it. Always remember: your health comes first.

> ### OFFICE GOSSIP MOTTO
>
> *'It's better to blow off steam than be powered by it.'*
>
> **MATTHEW CROSS**

CHAPTER FOUR
ALL WORK,
NO PLAY

BE YOURSELF, PLAY BY THE RULES AND WORK HARD

Everybody has to start somewhere. Remember that. Despite what you might read in the papers, with the tragedies, expectations and exploitations of the modern office intern, internships on the whole are fantastic opportunities to get ahead in business. But keep two eyes open and have your wits about you at all times, just in case. You never know what's around the corner, good or bad.

INTERNING – AN OVERVIEW

While there is much to celebrate about being an intern, the wider world is currently in two minds about unpaid internships. While I don't want to focus on these negative aspects too much – you've got enough to be worrying about, just surviving the day-to-day office – I should perhaps highlight some of the wider cultural context behind the ongoing 'Intern Debate'.

Currently, unpaid internships are receiving much negative attention, with many leading social commentators believing that internships are simply bad for business. The leading intern website, internaware.org (check them out) are also very suspicious of unpaid internships, because businesses believe the following to be true:

**GRADUATES NEED THE EXPERIENCE MORE THAN
THEY NEED THE MONEY**

WHY PAID INTERNSHIPS ARE GOOD FOR INTERNS

- They can provide a foot in the door across a wide range of industries.
- They provide valuable on-the-job work experience.
- They provide opportunities to 'test-drive' a career path before deciding on whether to commit.
- They give you a chance to establish contacts, to start networking.
- It looks good on your CV.
- You can accumulate new skills and experiences.

TO PAY OR NOT TO PAY

The average paid internship in the UK is around £19,000 – and that's for a one-year full-time internship. Many work-experience internships are unpaid – the interns are there to 'learn' and not 'work', and therefore, legally, don't require payment.

The promoters of UK-based internship programmes believe quite strongly that the whole point of an internship is that it 'isn't a job – it's an opportunity' and therefore doesn't demand wages. But what about interns whose internship placements require them to do work? What if they are unpaid?

In 2013, statistics from a survey on internship quality conducted by the European Youth Forum highlighted the following:

- 51 per cent of all interns surveyed had not been paid at all.
- 41 per cent of those who were paid found that the compensation level was insufficient to cover their day-to-day expenses.
- 25 per cent of the interns surveyed were unable to make ends meet.
- 65 per cent of all interns surveyed still relied on financial assistance from the Bank of Mum and Dad.

INTERN RIGHTS

As an intern, you have rights. These rights depend on your employment status. If an intern is classed as a 'worker' (i.e. they do actual work for the company, not just being trained or observing) then they're normally due the national minimum wage, at least.

Internships are sometimes called work placements or work experience. These terms have no legal status on their own, which makes some companies feel they can exploit interns by not paying them. The rights interns have depend on their employment status and whether they're classed as:

1. A worker
2. A volunteer
3. An employee

An intern is classed as a worker and is due the National Minimum Wage if they're promised a contract of future work. Employers can't avoid paying the national minimum wage if it's due by:

1. Saying or stating that it doesn't apply.
2. Making a written agreement saying someone isn't a worker or that they're a volunteer.

3. Work-experience students of compulsory school age, i.e. under 16, aren't entitled to the minimum wage.

If an intern does regular paid work for an employer, they may qualify as an employee and be eligible for employment rights. If your company has asked you to sign an employment contract then you're certainly an employee and eligible for pay. The employer doesn't have to pay the minimum wage if an internship only involves shadowing an employee, i.e. no work is carried out by the intern and they are only observing.

TYPES OF INTERNSHIP

There are many types of wonderful internships, just like there are many types of amazing interns. I assume, before you begin your internship, you'll know which one you are doing. If you don't, it's probably best you call someone up and check to find out what the hell you *are* doing.

PAID INTERNSHIPS

These internships are not as common as unpaid internships, currently – though you must double-check your rights. What type of internship are you doing? Are you employed by the company as a worker or are you volunteering your services? Which type of internship you are on affects your rights to payment.

UNPAID INTERNSHIPS

How long does your internship last?

A) One week ☐

B) Two weeks ☐

C) A month ☐

D) Three months ☐

E) 6 months ☐

F) One year ☐

G) Other ☐

Your rights to receive payment as an intern are all based on the terms of your employment and the duration of your internship. For example, a one-year internship programme is usually salaried, with the prospect of future work at the end of the internship with the same company outlined – though not explicit or guaranteed – beforehand. These internships are predicated on the company seeing a return on their investment – via the salary they paid you for 12 months – and eventually employing you as a member of staff. A one-week internship is based on work experience – a company may have a specific project they would like help with – and not likely to be paid, though expenses for travel and lunch are sometimes covered. I have no idea what type of internship you have but please make sure, before you begin, that YOU DO.

> *I love deadlines. I like the whooshing sound they make as they fly by.*
>
> **DOUGLAS ADAMS**

INTERNS IN THE NEWS

There always seems to be something in the news about interns. The last few years have seen a dramatic spike in interest in interns and internships.

But there have been a few particular stories recently that have really grabbed the attention of the world's media. The Internet has also suddenly (or at least it feels that way) become full to the brim with amazing intern stories of courage and bravery as well as, of course, dark tales of dishonesty and bad behaviour. Do yourself a favour before your internship begins and Google as much as you can about 'interns in the news' – get a feel for controversial stories as well as the achievements of interns who have gone above and beyond – and how.

In order to keep a balanced view of the rise of the intern in the media over the past couple of years, let's look at three intern-related stories that have shocked the world – one good, one bad and one ugly.

THE GOOD

You may remember this story – it was front-page news around most parts of the entire world. On 8 January 2011, an American politician, Gabrielle Giffords, was the victim of a shooting that saw six other people fatally shot and over a dozen seriously wounded while she was holding a meeting in a supermarket parking lot in Tuscon, Arizona, USA. Giffords was the victim of a near-fatal point-blank gunshot to the head. She survived, it has been reported, due to the quick thinking, bravery and basic medical training of her intern, Daniel Hernandez Jr. Giffords later praised her courageous intern as 'her hero'. Hernandez received a standing ovation, led by President Obama, at the memorial for those who lost their lives in the senseless shootings. Now, nobody is expecting you to quite literally stand in the firing line for your boss, but it should inspire you to know that there are interns out there who – in the face of immediate danger and shock – keep their cool and get to work. Mr Hernandez – we salute you, sir!

THE BAD

In the UK in September 2013, the fashion designer Dame Vivienne Westwood came under fire from a furious media – not to mention many disgruntled fashion interns all over the world – when her mega-rich fashion house advertised in a national newspaper for the position of five unpaid interns.

The internships, two of which would have lasted three months (and therefore deserved some financial remuneration), would have been attached directly to Westwood's wealthy London-based fashion house. The eccentric, super-loaded designer was attacked front and centre by many social commentators for not paying these interns, despite clearly having more than enough money in the bank to do so. Critics believed that Westwood was setting a bad example to other businesses.

Many newspapers criticised Westwood's appeal for 'volunteer' interns as a cheeky way of legally getting out of paying for labour, exploiting demand for such a job. Many hundreds of aspiring fashion designers applied for the coveted internships, despite the lack of a wage. The advertised role was five days a week, eight hours a day (a full day's work for most paid staff members, basically) and would have incorporated 'assisting' paid staff across many of the house's departments.

The internships, for which applicants were invited to send in a CV and covering letter, outlined that interns would undertake everyday office tasks, be skilled in computer programs like Word and Excel, and that some cover of 'reception duties' would also be required. So, work then – not shadowing.

Westwood's most recent media *faux pas* has fuelled the ongoing debate over whether interns (on a medium- to long-term placement) who are being asked to do a full-time job are being illegally exploited if they are unpaid – especially when the business has the means to do so. What do you think?

THE UGLY

One of the most horrifying tragedies in recent years concerning interns was the case of 21-year-old bank intern Moritz Erhardt, who was found dead towards the end of his seven-week placement for Bank of America Merrill Lynch, an investment bank in the City of London's financial district. Mr Erhardt, who had worked for 72 hours straight before his death, was reported as having said that he felt 'pressurised to succeed'. At the end of his 72-hour shift, the intern collapsed in the shower at his home. It was later recorded that he had worked through the night eight times in two weeks, getting home no earlier than 6am on many occasions, in an obvious attempt to impress his bosses.

Mr Erhardt's cause of death was reported as an epileptic fit, and the inquest into his death concluded that overwork could not be proved to be a contributing factor, but this sad and widely reported death brought into focus the stresses and business practices of interns in the office. Who is accountable for them and who is looking after them?

If you ever feel stressed or pressurised in your internship, there are many people you can talk to. You are not alone and, no matter what, don't ever be bullied into staying late regularly or working longer hours than you know to be healthy. Be confident of your rights as a worker and a valuable member of the team.

THINGS NEVER TO SAY IN THE WORKPLACE

You've made it this far. You've made it all the way through school, university and those very stressful interviews in order to get this internship. You've managed to wow, impress and excite your future employees so much that they have given you a chance to shine. This is your moment. This is your opportunity to show the world what you're made of. Please don't mess it all up now by opening your big mouth at the wrong time and saying something terribly insulting or inappropriate. It's inevitable, as the intern, that at some stage you will – but if you avoid these sentences below altogether then that's at least a good start.

- 'It was all her/his fault.'
- 'It's not fair.'
- 'I may be wrong, but...'
- 'I don't have time for this right now.'
- 'I'll try.'
- 'That's not my job!'
- 'But that's how I was told to do it.'
- 'I don't get paid enough to do this.'
- 'You're *how* old?
- 'Are you pregnant?'

QUOTES TO MAKE YOU SOUND EVEN MORE EDUCATED

We are all born ignorant, but one must work hard to remain stupid.

BENJAMIN FRANKLIN

BEST INTERN ADVICE EVER #6

READ THE NEWS Stay ahead of what's going on in the world. Impress your bosses and co-workers with your up-to-date news items. Casually drop titbits of recent news stories into your conversation. You don't have to understand what's going on (though it helps), you just have to recite BBC News tweets as if you do.

READING BETWEEN THE LINES

The modern workplace is jam-packed with poor, confused employees having to read between the lines of their managers and bosses, with their interchangeable decision processes, trying to work out what has been said and what was actually meant by it. As the intern, you'll not only have to navigate through steaming piles of hot smelly office politics, you'll also have to work out what somebody (usually your boss, or boss's boss) actually means when they've said something incomprehensible.

Here's a quick spotlight on deciphering office-speak – what is said versus what is actually meant. The quicker you learn this, the more effective you'll be, so keep up:

WHAT IS SAID	WHAT IS MEANT
'With the greatest respect'	'You're a moron'
'That's not bad at all'	'That's good'
'That's quite good'	'That's slightly disappointing'
'You're brave'	'You're mental'
'Can I suggest...?'	'This is how to do it'
'I hear what you're saying'	'I totally disagree with you'
'I'll bear that in mind'	'I've already forgotten it'
'It's probably my fault'	'It's definitely your fault'
'I only have a few minor comments'	'I've completely rewritten it'
'What else can we consider?'	'This idea is rubbish'
'I almost agree with you'	'I don't agree with you at all'

HOW TO MAKE SMALL TALK

Aside from gossiping, many interns will be judged, valued and ranked based on their ability to talk in, er, small talk. Workplace conversations are easy – if you're talking about work or are protected by your monitor, so no one can see your face. However, if you're talking to someone you don't know at all – in the reception area while waiting for a parcel to arrive, for example – then you'll have to rely on your burgeoning small-talk skills to get you past any awkward silences. These silences can be the death knell to starting new friendships in offices; an ability to ignite and hold a proper conversation is what will, ultimately, get people to like you. So here's a brief guide to starting and stopping small talk. Use it wisely!

HAVE APPROACHABLE BODY LANGUAGE
If your body language screams 'LEAVE ME ALONE', no one will dare engage in conversation with you. Shoulders back, back straight and head up – stand tall, not hunched – let people be invited by your presence, not threatened.

START WITH A FRIENDLY GREETING
You should start most conversations with the obvious 'Hello!' but always back it up with a direct question: 'How are *you* today?' or 'How's your day been?' Be friendly and engaging without coming across as desperate and needy. Difficult, isn't it?

KEEP THINGS POSITIVE
I tend to use lots of !!!!!!!!!!!! when I speak – it seems to keep conversations interesting. For example, 'Awful weather, isn't

it!!!!!' or 'I love tea!!!!!' This positivity will keep people engaged, if only in working out whether you're on drugs or not.

FIND COMMON GROUND
This may be challenging if the person you are talking to is 30 years older than you and owns the company, but give it a go. Music is always a good start. Try to gauge what they might be into and take some big swings – you might get lucky? This always works:

'What did you think of Lady Gaga's last record? YEAH, ME NEITHER.'

REVEAL SOMETHING ABOUT YOURSELF
Bonds are formed when people understand that you have nothing to hide and that you are who you appear to be. Revealing something about yourself – for example, that your parents are divorced or that you're allergic to nuts – makes people feel that you like them enough to trust them with that information. Once you've revealed a secret, and they reciprocate, you have sealed the first bond of friendship.

ENGAGE THE OTHER PERSON
One of the main reasons why friendships don't form in offices is because one person is always more committed than the other. Office friendships are partnerships – you have to engage one another, otherwise it all becomes a bit one-sided. If you find you're doing all the talking, then hold back, wait for the other person to speak. If they do, great, then listen. If they don't, then...

ASK QUESTIONS
Asking questions is a great way to learn new things about people without having to fumble around in inane conversation. It's also a great technique to get people to share information.

Questions about sport and music tend to go down best. 'Did you watch the game last night?' 'What's your favourite place around here to eat?' 'What did you do last night?' etc.

LOOK LIKE YOU'RE LISTENING

It's amazing how some people must think they look as if they're listening to you, when it's crystal clear that they're not. Some people get the 'dead eyes' so you can tell they have drifted off – they look through you rather than at you. Other people give off certain tells (such as turning away, or their hands becoming more fidgety) in their body language that indicate they've stopped listening. If somebody looks and sounds like they are not listening, throw in a few questions to grab their attention.

MENTION HANGING OUT AGAIN

If you like the person you're engaged in small talk with and feel like the conversation could, in the right setting, progress to 'big talk', then put your neck on the line and perhaps intonate, suggest or float the idea of maybe, you know, going out for a drink after work. This killer line always works: 'I'd like to hear your thoughts on that actually – do you fancy going to the pub later?' In one fell swoop you've been flattering, engaging, revealed something about yourself, asked a question and promoted a sense of continuation. Try it out.

FINISH STRONG

Always leave this piece of small talk on a positive note that suggests you look forward to doing it again. Make sure you say goodbye – though don't actually say the word 'goodbye'. 'Speak to you later' always works, as does 'Have a good one' and 'Catch you later'. If you finish the small talk strong it leaves the door open for possible 'medium talk' later on in the day.

FLATTERY WILL GET YOU EVERYWHERE

OK, this is it. This is the secret to how to really succeed in business. It's simple. It's easy. It's effective. It has no drawbacks. It works 100 per cent of the time. You can do it with your eyes closed. You ready?

The real key to your success as an intern is – *drum roll please* – FLATTERY.

Yep, the key to opening doors and becoming a successful intern, when we get down to brass tacks, is … flattering the hell out of other people. Plain and simple. Money may make the world go round, but it's flattery that lubricates it.

The thing with flattery is for it to appear natural, even if the recipient knows it's manipulative. The words have got to roll off your tongue as if you believe sincerely every word you say. Coming across as too sycophantic can do collateral damage to your career path, but there are subtle differences between out-and-out sycophancy and being flattering. You're the intern, so you'll have some wiggle room in the amount of flattery you'll be allowed to get away with, but don't overdo it. Litter your workplace conversations and small talk with as much flattery as you can stomach before having to violently throw up.

Here are some of my favourite items of workplace flattery – feel free to steal them, but please do come up with some of your own too. The more genuine they are, the more likely they are to be believed.

- 'Whose idea was that? It's great!'
- 'That dress looks amazing on you.'
- 'That was the best cup of tea I've ever had – thanks, Jenny.'
- 'John – that spreadsheet was the best!'
- 'Good meeting, guys – really enjoyed that one!'
- 'Have you lost weight recently – you're looking slimmer.'
- 'Your hair looks cool today – have you done something different?'
- 'I really enjoyed hanging out with you at lunch – let's do it again.'
- 'Many thanks for your constructive criticism – I found it really useful.'
- 'That's a really nice bag – looks really expensive.'
- 'Best. One-to-one. Ever. Thanks, boss.'
- 'I'm not as clever as you – could you help me out with something?'
- 'I can tell you're really good at your job.'
- 'You've got so much experience, but look so young.'
- 'I bet you got, like, five A-stars at school.'
- 'My IQ is 107. What's yours? Probably over 200, I reckon.'
- 'How do you stay so trim?'

... and so on, and so on. You get the picture.

BEST INTERN ADVICE EVER #7

Work out who the most popular person in the company is – and hitch your wagon to them. Become inseparable. The rest of your co-workers will follow.

MANAGING STRESS

Stress is nasty and stress is everywhere. You don't want it in your life. I can't *stress* that urgently enough (see what I did there, I threw in a bit of wordplay to lighten the mood).

'STRESS MANIFESTS AS A PHYSICAL, PSYCHOLOGICAL OR SOCIAL DYSFUNCTION RESULTING IN INDIVIDUALS FEELING UNABLE TO BRIDGE THE GAP WITH THE REQUIREMENTS OR EXPECTATIONS PLACED UPON THEM.'

You should be working hard, yes, but your internship should be enjoyable and free from the pitfalls of stress. A modern office is a breeding ground for stress. It can be infectious and specialised all at the same time. Be careful that stress never takes control of you on a daily basis. The odd bit won't hurt you, but don't ever let it consume you. And you'd be amazed at how quickly that can happen. Remember, IT'S JUST A JOB. If you feel stressed,

YOU'D NEVER GUESS - FACTS ABOUT OFFICES

Amazingly, the average office worker spends 50 minutes a day looking for lost files and other items that are no longer where they left them. This adds up to over four hours a week, or 194 hours a year – that's more than eight whole days.

overworked, underappreciated and full of work anxiety, don't bottle it up. Speak with the company's HR manager or with your intern placement supervisor immediately.

FACTS ABOUT WORKPLACE STRESS

I don't want to be a mood-hoover, but it's important you are aware – and understand – the potentially damaging effects of stress in a workplace.

- In the UK, stress affects one in five of the working population, from the intern to the board of directors.
- Stress is now the single biggest cause of sickness in the UK.
- Over 105 million days are lost to stress each year – costing UK employers £1.24 billion.

HOW TO CALM DOWN

Feeling stressed? Are you having the day from hell? Is the boss being a massive pain in the arse? Are you thinking of going on a mad rampage with a stapler? Don't. Breathe. Calm down. Sit down. Take a minute.

If you feel like today is just getting on top of you, just pause and relax. Take this book into the toilet. Sit down. Unwind your brain. OK?

Now clear your mind and just stare deeply into the pictures on the next page. Let them relax you – let them take you far, far away. Meditate. Breathe in and out. Declutter your mind from all distractions. Focus only on the images. Take your time – focus on one image for a few seconds before moving on to the next one. Feel your mind wander and drift off to another place. Let these images help you slip away to a place of tranquillity and peacefulness. Imagine you're a bird, soaring high, high above all your worries. Breathe. Keep looking until you feel at peace.

Feel better now?

HOW TO UNWIND AFTER A STRESSFUL DAY

I know from experience that being an intern is full of long and tiring days. In order to address your work-life balance (something only you can do), why not stick to my personal De-stress Plan. This plan basically involves treating yourself every single day, outside of work, so that you psychologically always feel like you're doing something good for yourself. While I was an intern I devised this chart – and every week I would swap the treats round so that I'd be enjoying a different treat every day of the week. Try mine out first – providing you like doing everything on it! – and then devise one for yourself. I guarantee it will de-stress you. Plus, you'll have something to look forward to every night ... which will make the day a bit more bearable.

DAY	TREAT
MONDAY	CATCH UP ON WEEKEND TV (very important)
TUESDAY	MAKE A FANCY MEAL (always something unusual)
WEDNESDAY	CINEMA / WATCH A MOVIE (take your pick)
THURSDAY	INVITE FRIENDS ROUND FOR SCRABBLE
FRIDAY	GET BLIND DRUNK (let off steam)

For the first couple of weeks of interning, this programme of treating myself nightly helped me reclaim my evenings as 'me' time. It's a great way to unwind and motivates you to work hard during the day so you can leave as close to 'on time' as possible so the evening is all yours. If you have to work late for a particular reason, or skip one of these treat nights, then make sure the next day you still treat yourself to something, be it a new pair of shoes or a run around the park (not necessarily a treat – but good for you). By doing so, you'll always feel like the work-life balance is more harmonious.

Feeling stressed and full of anxiety in an office job is one of life's most miserable certainties and, like death and taxes, you'll feel it nagging away at your soul every day. Only you can combat the stress in a way that helps you feel better. Some people take long bubble baths, some gorge themselves on chocolate, and others punish themselves at the gym. Whatever you need to do to unwind – DO IT. Otherwise, when the next morning rolls around, you'll feel exhausted before the day even begins and begin resenting the work you do as well as your co-workers.

CHAPTER FIVE
NICE WORK
IF YOU CAN
GET IT

YOUR CAREER LASTS 100,000 HOURS.
YOU'D BETTER GET CRACKING!

Work. Eat. Sleep. Repeat. Work. Eat. Sleep. Repeat. Work. Eat. Sleep. Repeat. And so on it goes for, approximately, the next 45 years of your life. But don't settle for being a wage slave just yet. Use the opportunity now to work out the rest of your career sensibly and smartly so that when you are asked 'WHERE DO YOU SEE YOURSELF IN FIVE YEARS?' you have a decent answer that you're actually happy with.

HEROES OF INTERNING: THREE INTERNS WHO CHANGED THE WORLD

Many notable people over the past 2,000 years started off as interns and apprentices. It has been argued that Jesus Christ was history's first ever intern. The Bible itself has this to say about it – 'Apprenticeship is the art of learning a trade sitting at the feet of the master'. Obviously, in the modern world you don't get ahead by sitting around at someone's feet, no matter how masterful they are. It takes blood, sweat and gumption.

Anyway, I'm digressing; here are three interns that changed the modern world.

1. STEVE JOBS

At the tender age of 12, Steve Jobs had his first office job at Hewlett-Packard. Jobs got the job when he cheekily phoned up HP boss Bill Hewlett, who was, rather surprisingly, listed in the Palo Alto phone book. But then everybody was back then. It was the 60s.

In an interview with *Playboy*, Jobs said, 'Bill got me a job that summer working at Hewlett-Packard on the line, assembling frequency counters. Assembling may be too strong. I was putting in screws. It didn't matter; I was in heaven. I remember my first day, expressing my complete enthusiasm and bliss at being at Hewlett-Packard.'

2. BILL GATES

Ol' Bill, or Young Bill as he was known back then, was still in high school when he got his first internship. Mr Gates (the richest computer geek in the world) spent his summer as a congressional page in Washington DC. His responsibilities included delivering messages, preparing the House chambers for each day's session and lots of other clichéd administrative tasks like filing, stationery orders and photocopying.

Funnily enough, when Gates was summoned to a Senate hearing years later (about the potential of a Microsoft monopoly), Ol' Bill reminded journalists of his time as a political intern and told them it was because of that that he stayed away from going into politics. The world is a better place because Gatesy started as an intern.

3. STEVEN SPIELBERG

This visionary director of such Hollywood blockbusters as *Jurassic Park*, *Jaws* and *Minority Report* started his professional life as an intern at Universal Studios, Los Angeles. While there he made his first film for theatrical release, the 26-minute-long *Amblin'* (1969).

When Sidney Sheinberg, then vice-president of production for Universal's television division, had seen the film, Spielberg became the youngest director ever to be signed for a long-term deal with a major Hollywood studio. Result!

EMAILS AN INTERN SHOULD NEVER SEND

This book is full of dos and don'ts while you journey through your days of being an intern. While I don't expect you to get everything 100 per cent right 100 per cent of the time, there are the absolute *musts* that you simply cannot get wrong. But don't worry, these are simple. Number One on this list is DO NOT SEND 'FUNNY' ALL-STAFF EMAILS TO YOUR COLLEAGUES. This is a no-no. In fact, this is a no-no-no.

For the first couple of days, weeks, and – to be safe – months, steer clear of any emails that might warrant any unnecessary suspicion about your character and/or personality. You may have the surging desire to fit in, express yourself and impress your co-workers, and get them to fall in love with 'who you are', and that's a good thing – don't repress that too much. However, your new friends should like you by you *just being yourself*. If you need to send viral emails or desperate emails to get other staff members to like you then, well, we should chat.

Here are a few email samples you should absolutely never send. Ever.

To: All Staff   **From:** Intern01
Re: MY LUNCH

Sorry for the All Staffer but whoever has taken my sandwich from the office fridge – could they return it immediately. The sandwich (cheese and ham) had a label on it designating it mine – I wrote 'INTERN' on it just to be clear.

If you know where my sandwich is, please let me know, I'm hungry. Thanks

Intern (hungry)

To: All Staff   **From:** Intern01
Re: FRIDAY VIRALS!!!!!!!!!

Hey everyone, it's Friday! CHECK OUT THESE FUNNY VIRAL LINKS my mate just sent me – he works for NUTS magazine. I'm pretty sure they don't have viruses attached!

Squirrrlfiringagun.com
Mangetshitbyatrain.gif
Surfersharkattack.avi

Enjoy!

The Intern

To: All Staff   **From:** Intern01
Re: NSFW

Hi Allan

My mate just sent me these NSFW links – thought you might like to see them!

BigoldBoobies.jpg
totallyNSFW.avi
donotopen.jpg

Fancy a pint at lunch time?

The Intern

To: All Staff   **From:** Intern01
Re: NSFW

Apologies for the all staffer.

I'd like to apologise for the email I just sent around – it was not meant to be for All Staff, it was meant for Allan Stafford.

My sincerest apologies. This will never happen again.

The Intern

OFFICE BODY LANGUAGE

Body language in an office is very important. As the intern you'll want to give off signs of 'non-verbal leakage' (i.e. body language) that tell others you're enjoying your job every minute of the day. Your body language, however, often gives off telltale signs that the opposite is true. Here are some quick tips on maintaining excellent body language – learn these and you won't regret it.

- Always extend a firm handshake – never offer a limp hand.
- Never invade other people's spaces – but do allow them to come closer to you.
- Never slouch. Sit up, back straight. Lean with your stomach, not your back, and keep your face looking calmly and confidently straight ahead, not down.
- Maintain eye-contact when speaking with someone – but not too much so that you look weird. My golden rule is: five seconds on, three seconds off.
- Keep your fidgeting to a minimum. You'll distract other employees if your squirming around becomes too apparent.
- Smile. Never frown. If you're constantly glum or look distressed, your fellow workers will assume you're not enjoying the work they handed down to you. And they'll take it personally.
- Don't shrug. Nobody likes a shrugger. According to experts, shrugging can undercut any message you are trying to convey in a conversation. So DON'T!

HOW TO MANAGE HAVING NO MONEY

Whether you're on a two-week work-experience placement, a three-month internship or a year-long, full-time employed post-graduate programme, the chances are you won't be earning much money compared to your friends or will be unpaid and have no income coming in other than what dear ol' mum and dad provide.

To help you, here's a few tips on saving, and making, some money while you are on your placement. They worked for me. It's not much … but every little helps.

- Buy a scratchcard (you've got to spend money to make money, am I right?)
- Buy your travel tickets in advance. And, if they haven't offered to, ask your placement liaison person if the company will pay for your expenses to and from work. They might say no, but it's worth a shot.
- Always go to the 'Reduced Items' section in supermarkets first. You might find a can of beans reduced to 11p – BARGAIN.
- Make your own lunches. When I was really skint, two slices of bread with brown sauce in the middle did me. And a banana.
- Look on the Internet for cheap deals and free events. Don't spend a fortune on cinema tickets and popcorn, visit the local art exhibition or free concert instead.
- Sell things you don't need to help you pay the rent. CDs, DVDs, you name it. Things you'll never use again? Put them on musicmagpie.com or gumtree.com.

- Websites such as freecyle.com or gumtree.com are brilliant for obtaining household items for free. I once got an upright piano from Freecycle for free and then later sold it for a profit. Cunning, eh?
- Cut up your credit cards. Getting into debt on credit cards will consume you. They may be good now, but they'll come and bite you on the bum later.
- Get a second job or weekend job. Work in a bar, on data entry, whatever you can get locally and keeps money coming in all helps. Plus, it's a great way to make new friends. I was a freelance music writer while I was an intern – I didn't get paid much but it got me out of the house.
- Never compare your lack of funds to your friends' wealth. They may earn more than you right now, but you are on your own path to enlightenment. And besides, money isn't the be-all and end-all – even though it might feel like it.
- Create a spreadsheet of incomings and outgoings – this'll help you save.
- 'Hello, mum. Can I borrow a tenner? I promise I'll pay you back.'
- Did I mention scratchcards?

BEST INTERN ADVICE EVER #8

At the end of your internship, don't cry.
Leave with dignity.

MANAGING YOUR FUTURE EXPECTATIONS

This is the question, no doubt, your mum and dad have been asking you every five years since you were five. And it's a valid question – where *do* you see yourself in five years?

Having a life plan that extends beyond the terms of your internship is important. It's no good working hard at a placement only to then sit on your bum for week after week. You need to capitalise on internships as the opportunities they are. If you're fortunate to be offered a full-time position at the end of your time there, then take that opportunity to reassess your life goals. Is this what you want to be doing with your life?

If, at the end of your internship, you are looking into a big black hole of emptiness where your career should be, don't panic just yet – use this time to look at where you can go next. Have a realistic look at what you can and can't achieve. Life is full of crushing disappointments – once you're an office jockey, a work donkey, a nine-to-fiver, you'll realise that pretty quickly. It's best to start managing your future expectations NOW, before it's too late.

In the table on page 124, choose ten things – professional and personal – that you'd like to accomplish in the next five years and try to work out how achievable they are. Then you'll be able to see in black and white a) what your long-term goals are, and b) how realistic it is to cram them all into a five-year period. It's time to manage your expectations realistically for future successes. The rest of us have had to, and now so do you.

PROFESSIONAL GOALS	REALISTICALLY ACHIEVABLE? (yes or no)
1.	☐
2.	☐
3.	☐
4.	☐
5.	☐
6.	☐
7.	☐
8.	☐
9.	☐
10.	☐

PERSONAL GOALS	REALISTICALLY ACHIEVABLE? (yes or no)
1.	☐
2.	☐
3.	☐
4.	☐
5.	☐
6.	☐
7.	☐
8.	☐
9.	☐
10.	☐

FREQUENTLY ASKED QUESTIONS

At the end of every internship, every intern has the same questions that require answering. Here are some of the most frequently asked, together with my answers:

What happens now? Try to get a job. My advice would be to apply sensibly for any role that you feel confident in doing well. Considering your new-found experience, skill set and office knowledge you should be much more desirable to employers than you were before your internship.

How do I get a job? The simple answer is: look everywhere. These days there are countless ways to find a job. That's both a good and bad thing. You'll have to whittle down the plethora of opportunities to what you think is realistic – and this is a big job in itself. Depending on what career you're hoping to follow, the areas to look for a job can either be broad or narrow. Your first port of call should be online – typing into a search engine what kind of job you want (and where) and seeing what comes up. Many newspapers have jobs sections that are inserted into them on a particular day every week – check the adverts and see if anything leaps out. There is no simple answer to this question. All you can do is manage your expectations realistically and sensibly focus on the areas and companies you'd like to work for and see what's available. If nothing seems to be available, you might have to re-evaluate your goals.

How do I survive without money? You don't. You'll need an income and you'll need one quickly. But the first thing to do is keep calm. There are many avenues to explore before you need to panic. First things first: draw up a budget in a spreadsheet and work out how much money you have, how long you can make it last, and tally up your income versus outgoings.

What if I need money immediately? While looking for your first permanent job, it is advisable to locate full-time or part-time office work (usually data entry) via temp agencies. Sign up at your local temp agencies – they will be able to find a role for you that hopefully matches the experience you have. After my first internship, my first job was plotting the flow of human waste on a map for water technicians to use when visiting people's homes. My second job was putting toppings on pizza in a factory. Not particularly thrilling, but they paid the bills until I found the job I wanted.

What are the best temp agencies? No matter where you live, there should always be a temp agency on your local high street. Google 'local temp agency' and a few should pop up. You'll need to complete a few (simple) tests but once you're on their books, work of some description should be quick to appear.

How do I find a good work agency online? Many industries these days have specific job agencies that locate roles from companies and find the right people to put forward for interview. If, for example, you want to become a web developer, use Google to find an agency that deals specifically with matching the right company with the right person for interview.

How do I apply for jobs? No matter how you have found your job to apply for, all companies will require your CV (which you'll update, now you have office experience) and a covering letter. There are many amazing books out there about how to write a decent covering letter. Or you could steal this one.

Dear XXX,

Having fought to the death for the prestigious [INSERT NAME OF INTERNSHIP] at XXXX, [INSERT YEAR] has been an intense year of hard graft and the constant smothering of elbow grease to my limbs. Transforming from a [INSERT DEGREE] graduate into an experienced, savvy individual in [INSERT LENGTH OF INTERNSHIP] has made me totally confident of my administrative talents.

My internship has strengthened my self-motivation and initiative, while giving me the ability to adapt shrewdly to various department strategies and techniques. It has taught me the value of my interpersonal skills, flexibility and to exploit my sheer love of pleasing people. These traits turn me into a reliable and indispensable member of any team. My software skills on formats such as Quark, Excel, Word, PowerPoint and Photoshop through to understanding [INSERT SOMETHING UNIQUE HERE] are impressive and demonstrate the speed at which I can learn, and adapt to, new techniques.

I have held the envied position of attending senior management meetings, brainstormed my own ideas with executives and had much successful and productive face-time with clients and customers. I am a quick learner with [INSERT EXPERIENCE LEARNED]. In addition, I am always the first in taking the initiative to make a great cup of tea should the throats of my fellow workmates run dry. I am a willing, dazzlingly enthusiastic and dedicated individual bursting with great ideas with the ability, unlike most, to time-manage my workload accordingly *and* organise a decent drinking session at any brewery.

From one look at my CV, you can see that [INSERT DREAM JOB] has been my future since I first flunked my Maths, Science and French GCSEs.

Thank you for your time. I hope to hear from you soon.

Kindest regards

[INSERT YOUR NAME HERE]

QUOTES TO MAKE YOU SOUND EVEN MORE EDUCATED

Choose a job you love, and you will never have to work a day in your life.

CONFUCIUS